The Art of Peace

The Art of Peace

*A Personal Manual on
Peacemaking and Creativity*

Stephen Longfellow Fiske

NEW PARADIGM BOOKS
Pasadena, California

The Art of Peace

Copyright © 1995 Stephen Longfellow Fiske
ISBN 0-932727-83-2 : $20.00

For information address:

New Paradigm Books
Hope Publishing
P.O. Box 60008
Pasadena, CA 91116 – U.S.A.
Telephone: 626-792-6123
Fax: 626-792-2121
email: hopepub@loop.com
www.hope-pub.com

Drawings Copyright © 1995 by Stephen Longfellow Fiske
Design and composition for this edition by Greg Endries
This book is printed with soy-based ink on 100% Kenaf tree-free,
chlorine-free, acid-free paper.

Printed in U.S.A.
2nd Printing 2001

*Dedicated to
the Peacemakers*

ACKNOWLEDGEMENTS

To my mother and father
who encouraged my artistic pursuits;

To my wife Nikki and our three children,
Evan, Elana and Amy,
who have been my daily teachers;

To Master Sivananda of Rishikesh
and his disciples, particularly
Swami Satchidananda, Swami Vishnu Devananda
and Swami Chidananda,
whose teachings have been so valuable in my life;

To my many friends, colleagues and teachers including Alan Cohen,
Rabbi Stan Levy, Ram Dass, Rev. Jim Conn, Louise Hay,
Jack Canfield, Ken Keyes, Jr., Ken Cohen, Marilyn Ferguson,
John and Dao Robbins and Al Huang.

To Gerda C. Fiske, Pat Proud, Dotti Albertine and Faith Annette Sand
for help in producing this work

CONTENTS

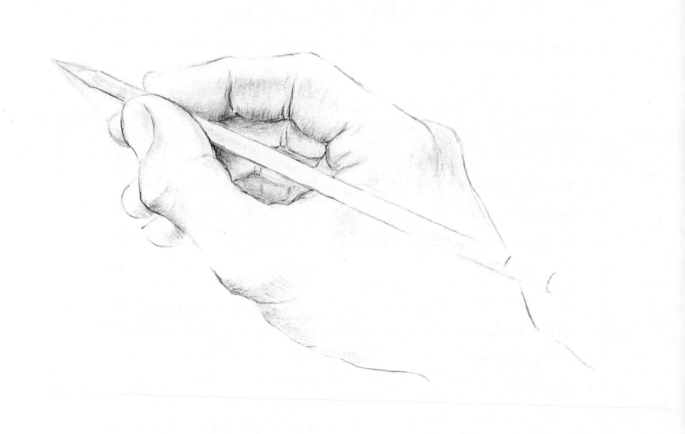

Foreword

by *Alan Cohen*

IN EVERY GENERATION there arises a chorus of voices that speak eloquently for the force of peace. Many of these voices are drowned out by the screeching of warmakers and some, like Christ, Gandhi and King, have been put down even as they speak. Yet all such visionaries leave noble seeds which grow and blossom far beyond the time and space that planetary healers walk here. Like blades of grass sending forth powerful shoots that grow far beyond the concrete that covered them, the song of healing rings for generations to come, calling all who have ears to hear the new yet ancient song.

It is especially meaningful when a voice is heard and acknowledged in the lifetime during which it speaks. When a man or woman of integrity brings forth a living message on the wings of sincere talent, the world is especially blessed.

Stephen Longfellow Fiske is such a one. A descendant of the celebrated poet Henry Wadsworth Longfellow, Stephen has picked up the threads of his ancestor's gifts and woven his own vision into a symphony of words, music and drawings by which the current generation is stirred.

Through my friendship with Stephen over many years, I am continuously moved and inspired by his dedication to service and planetary healing. Stephen is a committed, open-hearted, and high- thinking person who has offered his musical, artistic and intellectual talents to awaken the excitement for a new life on the planet.

I first met Stephen through his original "Earth Verse," a new addition to the tune of "The Star Spangled Banner." It had never dawned on me how

much the original words of the anthem glorify war. It took a new consciousness and a wellspring of courage to offer a new level of integrity to an
anthem of war that had not been questioned for over 200 years. My initial
reaction was, "Here is someone who is willing to make a heartfelt stand for
the highest values of the new world." I am happy to see that the new anthem
is becoming well-known and heard throughout the land.

The Art of Peace is a powerful and poetic manual for all who hold the vision
of a healed planet in our hearts. This articulate, poetic guidebook sets forth
the most important principles by which we may heal the pain that has beset
so many human beings, and establishes the foundation of the new world we
so ardently desire and need. Anyone seeking wisdom, support, and affirmation to hold the faith in the midst of fear will find a welcome companion in
this artistic and imaginative, yet sensible, book. Such a peacemaker would
do well to meditate on the noble thoughts contained between these covers,
and pray and practice to live them.

We are living during very challenging times; yet the opportunity for
healing is equal to the challenge. As Gandhi said, "The hatred of thousands
is offset by the light of one loving heart." You will find that light in The Art
of Peace. Such a force has a way of extending itself from heart-to-heart, until
the world becomes the one we cherish.

PART ONE

The Philosophy of Peace

Coming to the Peace Perspective

AS A CHILD growing up in New York City, I was exposed to a cross-cultured, diversified world. My parents had no particular overriding formal religious or ethnic traditions and they encouraged me to view the world with an open, creative mind. We were an artistic family, my mother having an opera/classical music background and my father being an editor/writer, so my imagination and creative faculties were admired and encouraged. In my world of make-believe, in my creative absorption in play, I first communicated with an inner sense of myself, made friends with myself and was completely lost in the joy of imagination, discovery and learning. I was blessed to have parents who nourished my inner child at play. I was thankful to grow up in a family that helped me discover who I am and to choose my own life path.

In my childhood, I found inside myself a sanctuary to which I could retreat and process the input from the world outside through fantasy, role-playing and imaginative play. From my adult perspective, I see in the child-at-play what I now know as the beginnings of my inner life—the ability to process feelings, to think through problems, to ponder questions, to envision and enter into creative process, to meditate, to pray, to affirm, to turn within for deeper spiritual connectedness and counsel and to know a sense of peace.

However, I also see that the child at play is in an open and vulnerable condition, easily encouraged and nourished, or frighteningly susceptible to rejection and hurt. I see how unmet needs and painful experiences that

1

remain unresolved from our past, repressed in our unconscious minds, can haunt and severely inhibit our experience in knowing happiness, fulfillment, love and peace. Our perspective and outlook on life becomes distorted by the weight of our past traumatic experiences and our old emotional baggage. My father's death from cancer, when I was 15, was such an experience.

I do not want to live my adult life with unfinished issues of my injured child festering—inside me. I want to heal and move on. I want to know my child at play, to know that sense of wonder, growth, discovery and creativity that makes life fun, purposeful and forward-moving.

To be enrolled in the art of living—to see our ardently sought-for vision becoming living, tangible reality—this, it seems to me, is the heart of adventurous, beautiful life.

As I experience the open state of consciousness and excitement of my creative activities, the joy and positive energy creates a safe place for my injured child to come out to play. By the forward momentum of creativity, I feel my playful self to be like a plant reaching for the light, nourished by the encrusted confines of seed and soil, but reaching beyond and not limited to them.

> I see playing as healing.
> I see the creative process as healer.
> I see creativity as the key to happiness and peace.

To be at peace with oneself and the world, to be healthy and whole, to be inspired by life and to fulfill one's dreams, to love, to enjoy and to be of service—these have become for me the cherished ideals to reach for in a turbulent, challenging world.

As my path unfolded and I became inspired by the lessons and teachings that came to me, I also became more in touch with an inner sense of guidance.

Over the years I began to write down in song, poetry and prose that which seemed most meaningful to share with others. This quest has led me to write this book, which has its premise in what I call "the peace perspective." This, for me, is a simple overview on which to base one's choices and to live one's life. While some of these ideas are not new, my hope is that in the manner in which I present this material they may be of meaning and benefit to you.

The Art of Peace is a philosophical and at times poetic discussion of the implications of this peace perspective through the focus of ten "peacemaker precepts." It is written as a personal manual based on general philosophical premises which can be adapted to specific life-styles and professional applications. *The Art of Peace* does not discuss the details of its potential relevance to politics, economics, education or even relationships, but rather it encourages the reader to consider these ideas and to use one's creativity in their specific applications. It is based on the idea that when there is clarity in one's basic premise and when our unique gifts of creativity are engaged in expressing that clarity through our actions and life-style, then we experience a sense of being on purpose, of living enrolled in mission along with the joy of manifesting our vision in reality.

Our ability to visualize and create to boundless dimensions is the greatest gift of the human species. If the premises from which our creativity springs are clouded by our fear, ignorance, intolerance, hatred, selfishness, power-mongering, emotional blocks and other "negative" controlling factors, then we create lots of problems for ourselves—the kind of global, societal and personal problems that we confront in the world every day. *The Art of*

Peace attempts to clarify a set of premises upon which to base our creativity towards manifesting a sustainable future of peace, justice, a healthy environment plus the nourishment of the dignity and beauty of each individual and of all life on our planet Earth.

The Art of Peace also recognizes that the "negative" factors—conflicts, obstacles and stuck places that come up in our creative endeavors towards peace—are actually an essential part of the creative process. We need to acknowledge the shadow side as well as the light. We need to recognize our warmaker tendencies as well as our peacemaker inclinations. We need to identify and come to terms with our ignorance, our blocks and our fears in order to move through them to grow and reach new understandings and levels of clarity. Living the art of peace embraces a holistic vision—where both negative and positive, fear and love, tiny cell and huge organism, the individual and the total population play integral parts in the balancing and healing process of creating overall peace.

The Peace Perspective

As we move into global awareness and confront the myriad issues that impede the process to peace, it becomes apparent that the basic premises with which we approach conflict must come from a perspective that takes into consideration these previously mentioned holistic understandings. In simple terms, the peace perspective is one where all choices and ultimate solutions in any problem-solving situations are based on upholding these following principles:

1. The unity of all life
2. Win/win understandings and solutions

3. The long-term good of the whole
4. Nonviolence
5. The fulfillment of our human/divine potential

These main points of the peace perspective are easy to say, but much more challenging to learn and live. Our history is one of disunity, of tribe and nation states at war with each other over political, economic, social, and religious differences. We've created a world of conquerors and vanquished, of allies and enemies, of winners and losers, haves and have-nots. Most of our choices have been based on exploitation and shortsighted, short-term gain carried out through violence and injustices among ourselves and plunder to our planet, its animals, environment and resources. Inherent in the peace perspective is a sense of balance and justice, a respect for the uniqueness and dignity of all inhabitants of this planet and the conservation and caretaking of our natural resources and vital ecosystem.

Our narrow doctrines of religion and cultural identities have bred fear and mistrust across our differences. Although most scriptures recognize an underlying oneness in all things, it seems radical and revolutionary to most religious thinking to embrace a concept that there is one universal creative life force (God) that moves throughout creation, which can be experienced within each of us as grace, truth, love, faith and peace. This life force is totally supportive of each seed, of each child, to reach its flowering and fulfillment when we cooperate and co-create with its Divine Will.

This creative energy of the universe is not out-of-reach or exclusive. Like the sun, it shines equally on the great and the small. It does not pick sides, blame or condemn "sinners." Through our free will and creativity it is ours to open to and know. Through our expanded consciousness, it leads us to tolerance, understanding, love, truth and faith.

The challenge of this age of accelerated progress, where our advances in industry and technology have outstripped our ability to use our creativity wisely and justly, is to change our way of thinking and living. This shift of consciousness begins within each individual but must be global in its ramifications, and must embrace universal and holistic premises: that we are here on this planet together; our survival and well-being depends on our commitment to make peace among ourselves and within our ecosystem.

Living from the peace perspective requires us to open up our vision wider than ever before, to reach deeper within ourselves to a universal heart, to the common ground we share with all peoples and our Earth. This is not easy when the grip of hate and intolerance is so strong in our world. It is not easy when much of our motivation is ruled by power and greed. It is not easy when our individual dysfunctional patterns prevent us from seeing this broader picture. It is not easy to heed the calling of the Peacemaker, yet this is our challenge.

I began writing *The Art of Peace* in 1984 when I was co-director of a Los Angeles/Santa Barbara-based organization called The Institute for Peace Studies. Early drafts of this book were used as a manual for our retreats and peace "boot camps" where the focus was on the integration of inner work with our outer activism for peace. This privately published, limited edition I never considered finished in its concept or writing.

As my musical career and family life began to require more of my time, I had to withdraw my labor of love energies from the institute. Despite numerous requests for additional copies, I placed the original version of *The Art of*

Peace in my desk drawer, vowing someday to revise and rewrite it. Over the years I jotted down relevant thoughts and inspirational notes in the margins and crossed out and rewrote portions. When the Persian Gulf War erupted, my energies became completely rekindled to focus on this book again.

Once again the voices of the peacemakers were drowned out by the clamor of the war drummers. Once again the tragic consequences were known to all the world, in untold human suffering, infrastructure destruction and horrifying ongoing environmental devastation. Once again it was graphically evident on television monitors throughout the world as we watched the day-by-day, play-by-play unfolding of events, that the insanity of war is not the way and that nations highly armed are nations highly unstable.

We have come to an age where war is obsolete. Now we must stop and transform the consciousness within ourselves that creates war and come to know, trust and implement a sane, secure alternative.

We are called into action—to extend outward into the world that peace we have come to know and embody within, which through our commitment and creativity, finds its way into the peaceful conversion of business, education, politics, and is the priority and basis of influence in society's institutions and social fabric. As we create this conversion within ourselves and our communities, we become an integral part of the critical mass of consciousness conversion on the planet, where from both the local and global viewpoint the unity and inter-relatedness of all things are primary.

We are called to create an alternative to the disharmonious and destructive direction our world has been taking. This alternative is based in universal values and principles such as those of the peace perspective and peacemaker precepts. These values form a premise, a grounding, for our creative alternatives.

From clarity of premise,

comes clarity of creativity.

Our creative exploration

opens new options,

so that we can see

the alternative

we never knew existed.

The alternative is found

within each individual,

in that sanctuary

where the inner child

can still be touched,

where our connectedness

to the wonders and beauty of life

can still be known,

and the joy of discovery,

the excitement of learning,

and the nurturing

of life's sacred blessings

are the focus of our living

and of our creative endeavors.

The old model of conquering and dominating must be replaced with a new model based on cooperation and an understanding of our inherent connectedness. It is a challenge that a new "army" of peacemakers worldwide must be willing to accept and be prepared to actualize on individual and collective grounds. It may be legitimate to claim that each nation of necessity needs to maintain a strong or adequate defense capability. But the old model of runaway weapon sales for profit and a simultaneous arms buildup beyond defensive needs is a sad and insidious travesty. The mad, the power-mongers of the world have no power if we do not give it to them, supplying them with the weaponry and technology they need to wield control through intimidation and authoritarianism. If we are not susceptible to their ideologies and policies, we will not make deals with them to benefit their short-term political, strategic or economic goals.

The security and stability of a nation is not found in the strength of its armaments, but rather in the character of its people. The foundation of a new model built by peacemakers is actualized through the efficiency and efficacy of its economy, in the justice of its laws and judicial system, the excellence of its education, the respected diversity and dignity of its people, the health of its environment, the wisdom of its energy and resource management policies, the integrity of its institutions, the richness of its arts and the vision and power of its creativity in the positive and peaceful use of technologies to build a prosperous, healthy and sustainable future.

All of this has to do with preparing a cultural context in which peace is possible. Although we can't anticipate what is to come, to accept that "crisis precedes solution" is a backward way of problem-solving. There must be some forethought, some preventative medicine in consciousness-raising.

Constructive action is needed before a crisis develops into something that gets out of control and results in devastating, emotionally wrenching consequences. We must learn to create transformation so that problem-solving methodologies and solutions preclude and dissipate crises. The peace perspective tackles issues in our world at the root cause of consciousness. *The Art of Peace* attempts to offer a new blend of psychologies and value systems helpful in assisting this transformation.

As a high school student in the early 60s, at New York's High School of Music and Art, I was deeply moved by the nonviolent tactics of Dr. Martin Luther King, Jr. during the Civil Rights Movement. Many of us at school were enrolled in supporting this movement, participating in marches and in singing songs of the times. I was impressed with the power of collective action to create change based on inwardly perceived and gut-felt ethical values of justice and human dignity.

At the same time, as a young person growing up in the intimidating streets of New York City, I was faced with the kind of "in-your-face" street confrontations and schoolyard battles that dictate how a man should react—not showing weakness or vulnerability but being tough and strong, not a wimp or a punk. Ethnic slurs, racist attitudes, machismo intimidation, gang affiliation, crime and drugs were all a part of my street reality. I learned to take care of myself, to walk the street walk. By being good in athletics I found I could gain respect and admiration from my peers.

Through the highly competitive world of intercollegiate athletics (basketball scholarship at New York University) I felt firsthand the pressures of the gladiator mentality—the other team is the enemy and winning is the only acceptable goal. At the same time, the upheaval of the 60s brought my

attention and involvement to political and social concerns. I felt the conflict and the alienation from authority. But when the coach said, "Go out and fight," I gave it all I had. In my mind the university, the team and the coach represented the establishment and a prescribed way of thinking and behaving that was expected of me, but from which I felt increasingly disenfranchised. I thought it was all screwed up. Fine young men in team blazers and short hair represented the American ideal, but there was nothing ideal about the madness of Kent State, Vietnam, Watts riots, political assassinations and the legacy of our institutions leading us astray.

Through involvement with Dr. King's nonviolence, reading Thoreau and exposure to Quaker values at the American Friends Service Committee, I came to study Gandhi's teachings of Satyagraha (soul force) and ahimsa (respect of all living things). These studies strongly influenced me to take the path of peace activism and conscientious objection during the Vietnam War.

My life took an abrupt change. I could no longer buy the company line. I took a vow of nonviolence in 1968, a vow which forms the cornerstone of the philosophy expressed in these pages. My life became dedicated to expressing my heartfelt concerns through the arts, so I went to San Francisco, joined a rock and roll band, embarking on my musical career.

In my involvement with peace activities in the 70s and 80s I saw a lot of "war" within the ranks of the peace movement as my well intentioned, but often enraged, peace-activist friends fought among themselves over issues of ego and control. It seemed difficult for them to talk to each other in ways that allowed a continued effective unity.

During this period I pursued my study of Gandhi's teachings and took a deep plunge into a practice of yoga and meditation. Through this I experienced a deepening inner peace. The same focus of discipline that I had used to become a good basketball player was now directed to a disciplined spiritual path where the goal was the realization of the Divine Self.

I also developed a keen interest in understanding methods of effective communication. I had seen enough of confrontational communication styles to know there must be a better way. It was painfully apparent that in any peace effort not only must an inner sense of peace be understood, but that communication skills, conflict-resolution techniques and formats that allow for honest, sensitive, respectful and efficient communication must be employed. Otherwise we get caught up in our reactivity, anger and frustration, create residual ill feelings and resentments and our progress can be damaged and delayed. We create win-lose instead of win-win.

It also became apparent that much of our traditional religious ideology and institutional thinking lags woefully behind the changes of the contemporary world and fails to comprehend the new holistic understandings and emerging ecopsychologies of a profound paradigm shift—which does not perceive the human species as sinners fearing a wrathful God. Rather, we are children of the universal creative life force, blessed with the gift of life. Our unique individual creative abilities and free will can harmonize and align with this creative life force (given the various names of God) as we evolve into a sense of enlightenment, fulfillment and peace.

God is within us and a direct knowing of our God-self is the inevitable result of an honest, disciplined spiritual practice and its creative application in practical, everyday living. The specifics of such spiritual practice vary according to the individual's choosing. A sincere and consistent effort will ultimately bring an upliftment and transcendence of consciousness towards peace and a compassionate, serviceful response to the world's woes.

While this transcendence is occurring, we are also coping with and rooting out through various psychological methodologies and programs those deeply-held emotional blocks and encrusted patterns and addictive behaviors that keep us apart from knowing ourselves and realizing this divine potential.

An additional aspect of this paradigm shift is the emerging understanding that the human species does not have "dominion" over nature in the sense of dominance and plunder, but rather that we are caretakers and stewards of our life-support ecology on this planet Earth. As tribal peoples have long understood, the Earth is our mother and nurturer. It is our sacred responsibility to honor, respect and live within her rhythms and laws.

I firmly believe that a root cause of our modern neurosis is our separation and divorce from our inherent and original relationship with nature. This rift, along with our conquering, exploiting and pillaging of nature's resources, has placed us in environmental peril. We have all heard the warning and each day wake up in a world at severe risk.

The environmental movement has done much to shift the consciousness to "green" awareness. The immediacy of the growing dangers, however, demand great urgency. The new environmental ethics and developing strategies to recognize and preserve our biodiversity and insure our sustainability must have a great ly accelerated impact on government and corporate policies, as well as individuals. If we are to change our  ways, take the necessary actions to heal the damage, preserve, conserve and leave a healthy future for our children and the following generations, we must act now.

Perhaps because I grew up in the city, apart from nature, and was influenced by my reading of Thoreau and Emerson, I felt irresistibly drawn to backpacking and to experiencing an intimate and vital relationship with the wilderness. This thirst for what I missed in the city has led me on my own vision quests—hiking and mountaineering thousands of miles through wilderness areas, at first in the Adirondacks of upper New York state, and then in the Sierra Nevada of California. I aligned in kinship with the spirit and teachings of Native Americans and with naturalist/author John Muir. It is in nature that I continue to find communion with what is for me an essential rapport with an undeniable part of myself—which guides me to an ever-deepening spiritual wholeness.

In this connectedness with nature we see that creation is an ongoing blending of masculine and feminine, resulting in the continuance of life. We come to know God the Mother as well as God the Father. Although each of us has a predominant gender, we are in holistic terms a blending of both masculine and feminine. Until the two come to a healthy integration within us, we are out of sync with ourselves. The patriarchal systems and the masculine dominance which has characterized our history has kept us in disharmony with ourselves, in our relationship with nature and with God. Those efforts to bring the feminine energies into a dynamic balance with the masculine are as significant a revolution as any in our history. It is an essential ingredient in our healing and making of peace.

My relationship with my wife Nikki has been a great continuing learning experience in this area of masculine-feminine balance. We are both breadwinners. We both have careers. We share responsibilities of home and children and are committed to parenting. We delegate tasks based on skills, ability, interest, need and availability rather than on prescribed societal roles. Decisions are made in discussion and consultation with each other. Disagreements and resentments are brought out in the open and worked through. Intimacy is rich, healing and deeply bonding. We are both committed to working out our problems and to truly hearing each other's needs without demanding or insisting on being right, in control or dominant. We both tend the garden of our lives together and are willing to work at the necessary tasks of weeding, pruning, watering, enriching the soil, planting and harvesting. It is mutual, respectful, sensitive and loving. It can be difficult, challenging and painful, but it is a balanced effort, a mutually supportive relationship and the most influential and rewarding experience of my life.

In addition to my years of adventure with Nikki and our family, my learning continues to be enriched and expressed through my continuing yogic practices, consistent involvement with peace, environmental and various humanitarian concerns and ongoing participation in consciousness-raising, human potential and communication skills training. My keen interest in comparative religion and philosophy and my own explorations of the creative process through musical, artistic and business endeavors also enhance my life. What comes out of all of this for me, as a handle to live by, is the peace perspective from which the art of peace derives.

The implementation of the peace perspective has its roots in the belief that the visionary factor of human consciousness and the creative process that manifests that vision into reality are what give life its most fulfilling meaning. The process of practicing peace is a lifetime commitment.

The specific practices that I employ in my own life are a synthesis of what I have learned works for me, plus what I am discovering every day and inventing as I go along. The "practices" that I include at the end of each precept chapter are meant to be guidelines and clues to inspire you to discover and invent your own exercises that will best serve you.

This is not a practical, how-to, nuts-and-bolts kind of book. Rather it is a book in which I attempt to clarify premise, expand vision and encourage the readers' creativity in their own unique application in their lives. Writing it has been a process that has helped me build a foundation from which to live my life and better understand how the nuts-and-bolts serve the greater function—the reason for living.

I realize that the portrait of the Peacemaker I paint in these pages follows the high road of philosophical idealism and spiritual premise. Like any seed that grows to blossom, we are here to fulfill our own flowering. It is this quest, this ideal, that drives the human species forward in creative endeavor. Without ideals, without vision, without the learning process and employment of creativity to achieve those ideals, life would be meaningless, devoid of adventure, hope and happiness. When an individual is absorbed in creativity, there is an opportunity for communion with divine inspiration and guidance from Divine Will. Without direct and personal interaction with one's own God connection within, spiritual life would be an empty, boring regimen.

In the end, *The Art of Peace* is a spiritual journey where I as pilgrim seek to be closer to God, to be an instrument of peace—to connect with other peacemakers and be of service in the healing of ourselves and the creation of peace in our world. I don't claim to be the ultimate peacemaker. I am only a seeker reaching for something greater. I am only an artist seeking fulfillment of expression.

Having made this effort, my prayer is that in releasing it, that it be of value to you.

Let us create a world where our children can play in peace.

There Is a Voice

THERE IS A VOICE IN ME that compels me to write, to sing, to speak out and share the inspiration, insights and heartfelt feelings that it conveys. When I close my eyes and am still, when I reach for the answers to my deepest questions, it is there to respond if I am ready to receive. It invites me to seek love, beauty, harmony. It invites me to live life fully, to reach the fulfillment of creative potential, to know the Divine Self.

It invites me to be healthy, to enjoy, to give to and serve others and to seek peace for myself and the world. There is a voice, I believe, within us all. Call it the voice of inner guidance, of conscience, of wisdom, of higher self. It is a voice that calls us forth to share our deepest heart and stand in the light of who we truly are. It is a voice that reminds us through trials, turmoil and tragedy that there is a purpose for it all. It is a voice of vision—of inspiration and direction to live that vision.

It is this voice that speaks in me as I write these pages. I hear it as a voice that speaks from a common heart—with a vision of peace that we all can see.

We all want peace, yet it eludes us. We protest, we rally, we fight wars in the name of peace, yet it still eludes us. Ours is a violent history, a violent world. Violence is easy to achieve. We are surrounded by it. Peace is much more challenging, more difficult to perceive. Peace looms as the shimmering hope on the distant horizon, the long-sought oasis in the desert of destruction. Like a mirage, it is within our sights, yet somehow slips away. Peace remains remote, mysterious, almost unknown.

Perhaps that which we know the least we fear the most.

Perhaps we fear peace.

Perhaps we fear what we might discover about ourselves if we really lived in peace. Perhaps we fear stepping outside of our separate, narrow identifications with the world (self, tribal, national, racial, cultural, religious) to face the possibilities of what a more expanded vision includes.

Perhaps we fear the more universal way of thinking, the integration and bridge building necessary to reach across differences and boundaries to come to peace.

Perhaps we are comfortable in our polarized mind-sets or comfort zones and fear the disruption that peace might bring.

Perhaps we fear letting go of some degree of power, position or advantage that we feel peace might threaten.

Perhaps we fear letting go of our selfishness, embracing the generosity and trust that peace requires.

Or are we so conditioned to our living in paranoia, hostility, deprivation, injustice, crime, exploitation, ecological disaster and mistrust that cynicism and hopelessness have become the norm beyond which we cannot see?

Are we so deeply in denial, apathy and disillusionment that we cannot rise above these limitations?

Are we so stooped with low self-esteem that we have lost self-initiative and empowerment?

Are we so under the thumb of government controls or bureaucratic regulations, dire socioeconomic conditions,

media manipulation and various oppressions that we feel
powerless to advocate and effect change?

Are we so conditioned and controlled by cultural mind-
sets and prescribed belief systems that we have lost our abilities of self-discrimination and open-minded exploration and
discovery?

Are we so used to intolerance that we cannot tolerate
peace? Are we victims and prisoners of crushed hope, blinded
by a violent and abusive world?

Perhaps the answers to such questions provide some of the reasons why
peace is so elusive. Perhaps we are neophytes when it comes to peace.
Perhaps we know very little about what it is and how to achieve it.

After all these centuries of bloody conflicts, we are certainly well-versed
in war making. We have numerous institutions dedicated to the art of war,
but where do we study the art of peace? Where can we go to have our peace
education and training, our peace boot camps, our skills in the mastery of
peace technologies honed and perfected?

We spend billions on weapons, war training and war related technologies, but what matching budgetary priority do we give to peace? What public dedication, what allocation of resources, what emphasis of human inge-
nuity and planning, commensurate with our war/defense effort, is given to
peace?

Where, when and how do we really give peace a chance?

Peace, it seems, has always been the road less taken, the uncharted territory. Is our preoccupation with violence, our passion for war, our lust for

blood, our zeal for the battle of competitive wills, an inherent human characteristic? There is a voice in me that says we have the capacity for peace, just as we have the capacity for war. And, we have the capacity for choice.

Peace does not occur because circumstances, events or environmental climate happen to allow for it. Rather peace begins within the individual. Individuals create the conditions conducive to peace and its ongoing maintenance. Peace is a choice. The art of peace is the skill with which we create inner peace and integrate that peace with our outer action.

In the holistic portrait of the peacemaker, peace is developed through practice and discipline and is reflected in every aspect of the individual's lifestyle. It recognizes the power of each individual to make a difference, and the power of collective, unified action to create transformation.

> I can only be truly responsible for myself and for the conditions of my own life. I can assist and influence you in various ways, but I can never be responsible for your behavior, as you could never be responsible for mine.
>
> I can take responsibility for being skillful in the manner in which I interact with others, so that those interactions can contribute to healthy, positive responses and results.
>
> I can take responsibility for the intent of my actions—that they be positive to benefit the long- term interest and good of the whole. I can take responsibility for listening to the needs and concerns of others without making demands, becoming reactive or insisting on my own agenda. I can take

responsibility for accepting feedback and criticism and adjusting my behavior.

I can take responsibility for recognizing and healing my emotional wounds.

I can take responsibility for confronting my own bias, fear, prejudice—and for making changes accordingly. I can take responsibility for the results of my action. I can have faith that every positive, life-affirming action made has a significant impact in our world. I can hold myself accountable for the degree to which I live my life in accordance with my innermost guidance.

In saying this, I also recognize that my actions contribute to the quality of life not only in my immediate sphere of activity, but in the rest of the world as well. I hold myself accountable for the effects my own negativity may contribute to the collective global consciousness. In this manner I also share in the creation of war, injustice, crime, poverty, intolerance and environmental damage. The tyrants and despots that arise are also the product of the world to which I have been contributing.

But as I take responsibility for eradicating these characteristics from my own life, I also contribute to minimizing and eliminating them from the world. As I align myself with others who are also thinking and living this way, we magnify our power and effectiveness through our collective action. As we assume a critical mass, we create change in the world reflecting that collective consciousness. Thus by creating peace in our personal lives, we create peace in the world.

Now more than ever, we must approach our individual lives and our global community from the peace perspective. In a world that glorifies the warmakers, we must accelerate our shift of awareness to handle the dangers and needs of a world where the speed of our technological advances has outraced our ability to manage them wisely. We must define for ourselves what peacemaking really is and become peacemakers.

Peace is a new way of thinking. Peace is a new way of living. From the peace perspective comes new economics, business, politics, values, technologies, institutions, art. We have barely scratched the surface. The boundaries of the field of peace are endless. Peace, as a whole frontier of human exploration and endeavor, awaits and offers us the challenge and prospect of a healthier, brighter age.

For peace to work, it must offer us a better sense of security than the conqueror mentality/weapons buildup/warpath approach. For peace to exist, basic human needs must be met. In addition to the need for adequate food, clothing and shelter, there must be a sense of security from the fears of crime, hate, intolerance, oppression, injustice and disease. A "peace" that is based on fear, threat and mistrust is not a secure peace, only a tense suspension of hostility while preparing for the next battle.

How can we have peace when so many of our resources are squandered on weapons, war and defense activities instead of serving basic human needs?

How can we have peace when starvation, poverty, crime, injustice and disease are rampant in our world?

How can we have peace in the face of unspeakable human rights violations and atrocities?

How can there be peace in an environment polluted and pushed to the edges of ecological devastation?

How can we have peace without learning how to settle disputes in nonviolent ways?

A secure and lasting peace must not only serve our sense of outer safety, but must serve our inner needs—for purpose, self-respect, dignity and spiritual sustenance in life. Peace begins within. Without the establishment of an inner sense of peace, the issues and tensions that plague us, uncured like a disease whose symptoms have been temporarily suppressed by drugs, will fester inside and reoccur. The art of peace must include a strong dose of preventive medicine that goes to the root of the problem and helps each individual and situation heal from within. At that point our peace can emerge from our inherent foundation already whole and be sustained through our positive creativity.

We human beings, unique in our creativity, must have vision—a channel for our inspiration to move through and reach an ardently sought-for greater aspiration. When there is a sense of art to our lives and we are absorbed in creative endeavor, life becomes most enjoyable and fulfilling. We are all artists in that we are enrolled in creating our lives and the conditions in which we operate. The question is, are we in charge of our lives—or are we victims under the control of other powers or insurmountable circumstances?

The person of vision, of creativity, is at cause and is enrolled in the mission of achieving that vision. Life is challenging, forward-moving and worthwhile.

Any art endeavor includes various elements of vision, challenge, skill, discipline, technique, individuality, style, improvisation, risk, questioning, focus, rendering of form, using of tools and achieving results. Ultimately it is our lives and our world which we are scripting, painting, orchestrating, conducting, acting, directing and dancing.

How do we want the script to read? How do we want the picture to look? How do we want our role to be played? What kind of impact will we make? How do we want our contribution to be reviewed and remembered? What do we leave for our children's legacy?

There is a voice in me that tells me that peace is what the people of the world want more than anything. If we can see peace as an art, a skill, then perhaps it becomes more accessible. Like any art form, peace takes practice.

If you want to be good at war, you study and practice the arts and skills of war.

If you want to be good at peace, you study and practice the arts and skills of peace.

By Being a Peacemaker

Peace?

Can we really know peace
in this world of distress?
Is peace just a fool's wish
that poets address?

Are we hopelessly bound
by war's travesty
like lemmings
helplessly bound for the sea

or can we rise
to a new destiny?

Has not history's rampage of war
made it clear
that the quest for peace
is the next frontier

and the maker of peace
the new pioneer?

Peace?

It seems rare,
elusive,
this peace

yet it is inherent
everywhere

within
the stillness of the heart

throughout
nature's symbiotic design

patiently calling from the soul

peace is

already here

already ours
if we would but awaken

to its presence

There is a peace powerful
there is a peace glorious
there is a peace majestic
which moves through the mountains and sky
and resounds throughout the splendor
of nature's magnificent and mysterious creation

It pounds in the surf
sifts through the sand
sings in the wind
is felt in the warm touch of a hand
is known in the silent stillness within

There is
a peace that nurtures
a peace that sustains
a peace that heals and restores
a peace that unites
a peace that rejoices
a peace that brings faith
in laughter
in tears
in joy
in a sigh
in sorrow
in forgiveness

There is
a peace in birth
a peace in death
a peace in sleep
a peace in awakening
a peace that opens the heart
quiets the restless thoughts
and saturates the soul

A peace so powerful
we are humbled in its presence

A peace so powerful
that all our needs and deeds
are but grains in the sand of its tidal time
washed and rolled
turned and turned
again and again
surrendered in its current

We don't need to run after peace
but to accept it.

We don't need to protest for peace
but to live it.

We don't really need to "make peace"
but to choose it.

We don't need to end conflict
but to understand peace.

Now more than ever, let us build bridges
and create new possibilities
for ourselves and our world
by being Peacemakers
by knowing peace
by practicing, exemplifying
and teaching peace.

Peace is many things to many people.
To some it is the absence of war.
To some it is a stable economy,
or a sense of national security
and military strength.

To some it is an inner strength,
an inner sense of balance, of harmony
of wholeness, of health
of happiness, of vitality
of spiritual fulfillment...
a serenity of consciousness.

Others may equate peace with boredom.
To some, peace may mean weakness,
acquiescence, non-machismo.

To others it may be a desired status quo,
an absence of agitation or anxiety,
a calm, an ease, a comfort zone.

To an aesthetic or renunciate,
peace can be found in desirelessness,
in withdrawal from the material and sensual lures
of the world.

To others still, peace may be a source of power,
of renewed inspiration and faith.

To some, peace may be an agreement,
a pact, terms,
the result of a pragmatic, step-by-step process
involving the use of diplomacy,
mediation, arbitration
and conflict-resolution methodologies.

To others peace may be just an idea
a distant concept or a dream.

Peace may be all these things and much more.

Words could never fully define
"the peace that passeth understanding"

We all want peace, but how?

By being Peacemakers.

As Peacemakers we may know peace as a skill
a process
a way
an art .

The art of peace, the process of peacemaking,
is the art of living harmoniously
on all levels of existence
so that peace becomes an experience
that moves beyond concept
to a living reality;
a presence, an embodiment
that comes by practicing and doing,
by actualizing
by basing our choices on peacemaking precepts
and being creative and dedicated enough
to improvise and implement those precepts
through our choices
and anchor them to our action
for the long-term interest
and the good of the whole.

The art of peace begins
in the heart of each individual
with the desire to be at peace with oneself
and extends to the common heart
of the family of humanity
with the desire for peace on Earth.

Peacemaking is the art of creating our lives
and the conditions around our lives
in a way that supports the well-being
of all life.

Peacemaking is the art of relating to
and handling conflict in such a way
that we do not become at odds with life
but are rather in sync
and able to manage constructively
whatever changes and challenges life offers.

Peacemaking is the art
of accepting conflict and dispute
as an inevitable occurrence in life's experience
and embracing the challenge
of facilitating such events
for the most equitable and beneficial outcome
or resolution possible.

Peacemaking is the art of finding
the common ground and common heart
in any situation
and seeking a win-win understanding.

Peacemaking is the art
of opposing violent solutions to solving problems
and offering and substantiating
alternative nonviolent solutions
as credible and appropriate.

Peacemaking is the art of living our lives
in a dynamic state of strength, balance,
love, integrity and faith
so that our full, creative potential as individuals
as community, as nations, as a planetary people
is realized.

Peacemaking is the art of perceiving
the universal spiritual connectedness of all peoples
and finding a way to bridge differences
and create bonds that transcend fear.

Peacemaking is the art of actualizing peace
on all levels of living.

We can choose to create an atmosphere
of fear and enmity
or we can choose to create
a more harmonious reality
where a context conducive to managing differences
resolving conflicts and settling disputes
in a collaborative, nonviolent manner
is achieved.

My conscience does not accept
any feared, inevitable, ultimate catastrophe
nor will I be a silent partner
in the perpetration of the unconscionable.

I must act. I must speak out.
I must let my voice be heard.

As I look into my children's eyes,
bright, alive, trusting, hopeful,
I know my spirit is too much alive,
too filled with hope
to seek other than hope's horizon...

But it is more than hope
that we need as Peacemakers
to transform the deep programming
of centuries of war consciousness...

It is the development of a new way
of thinking and living...

By being Peacemakers
we place peace as the priority
of our lives and our time,
revising the very way we perceive the world
and the way in which we interact
on all levels.

By being Peacemakers we take part
in weaving a whole new societal structure
on the loom of peace
where we develop the skills and disciplines
of the art of peace, and teach it
to ourselves and our children
starting with the thread of each individual
and weaving it into the collective fabric of society.

We give the subject of peace a priority place
in our educational system and public institutions
alongside math, history and science
from elementary school on.

As our leaders become educated and practiced
in peacemaking, and their decisions reflect
the peace perspective
resulting in new societal building blocks,
then peace begins to take shape in our society
as good economics, good politics,
good communication, good sense.

By being Peacemakers
we call for unity of spirit in the common interest
of our very own survival and well-being
and we recognize the significance of each individual
as the integral part in creating the shift to peace.

It is up to each one of us to choose
how we want our lives and our world to be.

If

by being a Peacemaker

I am judged

a wishful poet

a cloud-built philosopher

a fool

a dreamer

a blind believer

a hopeful perceiver

then I would choose

to live my last breath

as all these things

by being a Peacemaker.

PART TWO

Making Peace a Reality

The Peacemaker Precepts

Affirming Unity

Managing and Resolving Conflict

Nonviolence

Protecting All Life

Make No Enemies

Living by Truth

Living by Love

Living by Faith

Integrity of Will

The Creative Process

Affirming Unity

A Peacemaker creates no separations
but seeks always the unity,
the common ground,
the common heart,
the common purpose of life itself
of survival and sustenance
of preserving and nurturing life's
sacred seed
from the source of creation's miracle
to the flowering of its fulfillment,
through the continuance of life's eternal attempt.

A Peacemaker sees that the universe
in its myriad diverse forms and patterns
is a unity,
an orchestrated, choreographed whole
in which there is nothing so great or so small
that does not in some way interact
with the parts of itself;

that all of life is in symbiotic relationship
within the ecosystem of itself;
that what happens anywhere
affects what happens everywhere
so that whatever we choose
affects the whole of the world.

Knowing this
a Peacemaker affirms this unity
inwardly
as wholeness, as spiritual unity,
as oneness with God,
and outwardly
as unity with all of nature and all people.

As a citizen of the community of the planet Earth,
a member of the human family
united in one common spirit,
a Peacemaker affirms unity
as the foundation of peace.

Practices

1. Go to a place where you can feel a sense of raw nature, away from the buzz and hubbub of everyday civilization. Make a physical connection with the Earth, whether by feeling the wind or the soil underfoot, by touching a tree or taking a rock, a flower or a pine cone in your hand. Be still. Allow your mind to release its thoughts and concerns, if only for a few moments. Feel your connection to nature. Connect with the unity of all creation. Know that you are nourished. Know that the creative energy of the universe moving through you is the source of inspiration and creativity. Become an open channel for its passage.

Try to make this connection as often and as regularly as you can. In these visits with nature, with God—however it is that you perceive God to be— and with yourself, you will draw a sense of replenishment, of healing, of connectedness, a spiritual upliftment and a positive and powerful vigor for living. The deeper you take yourself into this experience, the more you will come to an inner sense of peace.

2. Go to another person—a friend, a lover, an acquaintance. Before your interaction with this person, take a moment with yourself to prepare yourself and commit yourself to having more than a casual, superficial experience.

Affirm inwardly that you are going to experience a heart-to-heart communication. You are going to touch someone in a meaningful exchange with a positive word, an encouragement, an acknowledgment. You are not separate or alienated from this person. Put any resentments and animosities aside. Be open to listen. Be open to learn. Respond with interest and support. Share a bit of yourself. Seek to connect. Seek a unity. You will receive in return what you give.

Affirmations:

I am one with the Earth and the sun.

I am one with all life.

The creative energy of the universe is flowing through me in every moment.

I am an integral part of creation.

I am a magnificent, unique individual.

I am an important and valued member of the family of humanity.

I am a contributor to peace.

Managing and Resolving Conflict

Established in unity,
no matter how vast differences may seem,
no matter how inflexible or intransigent
the positions of the parties involved may appear,
a Peacemaker's goal is for all conflict
to be managed and resolved nonviolently,
minimizing loss, maximizing gain.

A Peacemaker seeks not to be an agent of conflict,
to make demands, issue ultimatums, place blame,
insult or indulge in inflammatory remarks or behavior,
but to remain as centered and nonbiased
as possible and to establish an agreed-upon
means of operation or process
through which to deal with conflict,
and then through that avenue
establish degrees of tolerance, rapport, respect,
cooperation, compromise, collaboration and trust,
leaving the conflict manageable or resolved
and laying the groundwork for possible
partnership, friendship or alliance to result.

By affirming a basis of unity
rather than emphasizing differences,
we first establish grounds of common purpose
for our mutual self-interest
and the good of the whole.

Whether we are a party in conflict,
a mediator or facilitator,
a leader or a follower,
a star or a bit player,
we need to see that we are not alone

We need to see ourselves as a team.

Any experience of team-building
or group movement towards a common goal
is based on individuals understanding and
overcoming their conflicts and limitations,
whether within themselves or with others,
and reaching for the fulfillment of their potentials,
both individually and collectively.

This challenge draws out our resourcefulness
and motivates us towards creating a unity,
where the whole is greater
than the sum of its parts.

In this team-building model,
the strengths of each individual
compliment and enhance the other.
The weaknesses of each individual
become recognized, worked with and placed
into the best possible balanced context of the team.
Clear roles are established
based on collaboration for the good of the whole.

We are all in this together.
You and I are us.
I am not versus you. I am with you.

We are on the same team.
There need be no winner and loser.
We can both win.
We can mutually benefit from the peaceful
and just solution of our conflict.

We begin by recognizing that each side
has a point of view
that must be acknowledged and heard.

The successful management and resolution
of our conflict
require that we really hear each other
and acknowledge that we have listened
and have truly heard the other side.
We don't have to agree, but to truly listen.

By listening
we try honestly to see the other point of view,
understand it as they perceive it
"get into their heads," "get behind their skin,"
"see through their eyes," "walk in their shoes."

By listening
we begin to break down the polarized positions.

By listening
we begin to create an atmosphere of receptivity,
of acceptance, of acknowledgment,
an atmosphere of us.

By creating an atmosphere of us
rather than a confrontational, competitive,
combative context,
we are beginning to communicate meaningfully.
The walls are breaking down
and we are beginning to trust.

If, however, one or both of the parties
are so polarized and filled up
with their own argument
that there is little or no room to truly listen
to another position,
then direct communication may not be possible.

In this case,
we may employ a process
which allows for the opposing parties
to express their positions and agendas
to a third neutral party or negotiating team.
The opposing parties, who can't talk to each other,
talk to the third party,
who acknowledges each respective position
as heard and understood.
The opposing parties can,
through the safe matrix of the third party,
release the weight
of their positions and agenda
and spill out
pent-up emotions, passions and frustrations,
without the fear of face-to-face reactivity.

When the third party has communicated
the opposing positions to each respective party,
and each understands
that they have been heard and acknowledged,
then there may begin to be room
to be receptive,
to listen and seek understanding
of the other point of view.

In such cases,
where the parties might not even want to be
in proximity to each other,
the procedure can be tedious, laborious,
sometimes very tense and painstakingly slow.

A Peacemaker must cultivate high degrees
of patience, perseverance
and sensitivity to others.

Well-cultivated, deeply ingrained,
long-standing barriers do not easily fall,
yet it is such fear-supported barriers
within ourselves and throughout the world
that must be overcome to achieve peace.

In any circumstance of conflict management
and resolution,
reducing fear and establishing trust,
even to a minute degree, is the key.

Once we are communicating
with a degree of established trust,
we can start to look at our differences
for mutual understandings
and areas of possible compromise, collaboration
and/or agreement.

Agreeing to listen,
listening,
and acknowledging what you have listened to
are the first steps in establishing trust and rapport.

Listening requires
that we do our best to set aside bias,
step back from our position,
focus just on what is being communicated,
and then acknowledge what we have heard
from the other point of view.

When we focus on just listening, rather than
judging, reacting or preparing to respond,
a communication bridge is built
for sending and receiving,
interconnecting and exchanging,
which then helps diffuse our polarization,
so that mutual understanding and trust
can be encouraged and enhanced.

When we have been listened to,
and the grounds of trust become established,
then we begin to feel more secure
to open up, share positions and feelings,
and to react less defensively and hostilely
towards each other.

While it is healthy to express
our frustration and rage,
it is healthier yet to create a context
where such venting can bring constructive results.

We can agree to disagree with respect and dignity,
without rejecting the other party's right
to express grievances and positions.

Our differences can be beautiful,
and the communication and understanding
of our differences
can be a wonderful and enlightening experience.

Difference, and ensuing conflict,
is an inevitable consequence of our living.

A Peacemaker sees the underlying unity
and understands and accepts difference
as a marvelous reality of our diversified world.

A Peacemaker respects differences
and acknowledges that while differences
may not be resolved,
resulting conflict can be managed.

A Peacemaker learns to embrace conflict,
to welcome it as a challenge,
to employ our creativity
in the opportunity to grow and learn
how to transcend and transform crisis
into the best solution possible.

When we know that our respective feelings,
positions and agendas have been heard,
that direct responses are being received,
and that new mutual understandings and pacts
are possible and in process,
then our differences become
increasingly more reasonable to bridge.

A Peacemaker learns
to minimize intolerance, intimidation,
mistrust and fear,
by creating a respectful context
where suspicion, threat, alienation
and all forms of separating modalities
can be safely addressed and worked through.

All of this, of course, is assuming that the parties involved are willing to make a reasonable effort to come to the table and engage in a conflict-resolution process at all. Part of the skill of a Peacemaker is to determine what methods, what avenues of inquiry, what kind of pressures, what tact of diplomacy, what sense of timing, what strategies can be employed to bring a reactionary or unreasonable party to the table, short of a court of law.

In all phases of the process, a Peacemaker makes the best effort to facilitate a communication circuitry which allows for an honest and creative give-and-take, leading to a new understanding and resolution based on the peace perspective.

As we become skilled
at managing and resolving conflict,
so that step-by-step our conflicts become
better communicated
better understood
better negotiated
better managed
better resolved,
we see our peacemaking process,
our peace pacts with ourselves and our world,
opening new doors, new possibilities.

Each time we have opposing sides
we are offered the opportunity
to create the magical experience
of a new paradigm, a synergy
that is better for both sides together
than it was apart.

Practices: Listening

We are so used to arguing, being defensive, being reactive, competitive, preparing our response, insisting on being right, that we rarely truly listen. To be a good listener is a skill that takes patience, discipline and control.

Next time you are in a discussion, debate or disagreement, practice holding your tongue, practice not preparing your own responsive argument, practice controlling your reactivity, your potential anger or hostility, even though you may be under attack or in strong disagreement. Practice recognizing and controlling your own bias, your own closed-mindedness. Practice not insisting. Practice really hearing what the other point of view is all about. Then practice acknowledging that person for their point of view, so that they know they have been truly heard and that their argument has at least received the respect of being listened to, even if they know you disagree.

As you practice your listening skills and begin to improve, see if the quality of communication with others isn't also improving. If you become good at listening to others, then others will listen to you.

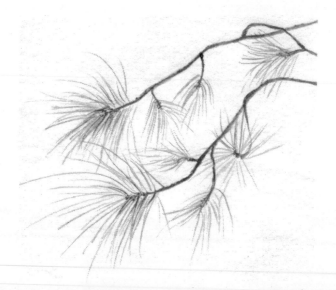

Affirmations:

I am a partner with every human being.
I am uniquely different and essentially connected
in heart and soul with everyone.
I am able to recognize differences and to build bridges of understanding
in my relationships.
I am capable of creating boundaries of respect and rapport
in my relationships.
I am able to listen and truly hear another person's point of view.
I can manage or resolve conflicts in my life.
I can express myself with clarity, honesty and love.

Nonviolence

A Peacemaker practices nonviolence
in thought, word and deed.

A Peacemaker shuns the use of violence
in any circumstance.

Violence is any act which is intentionally
harmful, abusive or destructive of life.

VIOLENCE IS COMMITTED for the sake of violence and can also be done against property and resources where the intent is to be harmful, or damaging to life-support systems and infrastructures.

Violence may not just be a physical act, but could also be verbal attack, harassment, discrimination, threat, intimidation or emotional depravation—wherever the intent is harmful or abusive of basic human rights, needs and dignity.

Because thought and word precede action, and violent intent precedes violence, a Peacemaker seeks to find the root cause of violence within. Violent thought or vengeful motive carry the seeds of violent action and can be considered intrinsically violent in that they are suggestive of violence. It is but a short step when suggestive violence aggravates itself into physical violence.

War is the extended action of widespread violence,
whether carried out by an individual or on a collective basis.

Nonviolence holds all life sacred,
is love and respect for all living things,
with no intended harm or injury to anything.

Nonviolence upholds the sanctity, dignity, beauty, love, power and grace
of the human spirit and all God's creation.

In the face of a violent world,
nonviolence is the response of inner strength
and the commitment to the deepest moral, ethical and
spiritual values and principles.

A Peacemaker knows that violent thoughts and actions
create an atmosphere of fear and unrest
provoking discordance and violent retaliation.

Violence perpetuates violence.

The roots of violence are ignorance and fear.

The basic ignorance is not knowing our unity, our oneness,
our common heart as the family of humanity,
sharing the resources of the Earth and its fragile ecosystem.

We are ignorant because, although we have information available to us, we don't know how to find or use it. We have sources of support where information, knowledge and resources could benefit our situation, but we fail to use what we have because of lost self-initiative, apathy, cynicism and lost hope. We fall prey to misguided leadership and the failure of powers that be to understand the true nature of everyday problems and basic human needs. We allow ourselves to become victims—oppressed and denied opportunity.

The basic fear is rooted in blindness to the truth. We are afraid and we mistrust that which we cannot see, have or understand, or we mistrust that which we choose not to see, have or understand.

Social, economic and political injustice—all basically rooted in ignorance and fear bred in the societal system—create want, indignity, shame and suffering, resulting in a high incidence of deprivation, alienation, crime and the breakdown of our security as a society.

When there is unequal access to, and unequal distribution of, resources, goods and services, when people are oppressed and suffer injustices while others are privileged and exceedingly affluent, there is great danger of widespread ignorance and fear on all levels of society, whether in white-collar circles or on the street, whether in "good old boy" networks or in gangs.

When people feel powerless and frustrated, as the result
of racial, class-based, or various political inequities,
and the justice system itself is fraught with bias
within its own ranks,

handing down continuous decisions which lose the
confidence and trust of these people,
then there is bound to be an increasingly disenfranchised,
entrenched and enraged section of society
simmering in fueled conditions for civil unrest.
It is inevitable that desperation leads to desperate acts.

The haves fear losing what they have,
and fear the have-nots for wanting what they have,
become protective and exclusive
and so try to keep the have-nots down.
The have-nots fear the continuation or worsening of
their have-not condition, become apathetic and cynical,
and resent and place blame on the haves.

Ignorance,
exacerbated by an often polarized and biased unwillingness
to face the realities and problems across boundaries of society,
is fed by alienation and mistrust.

Confounded by a lack of skill in conflict resolution
so that meaningful communication is difficult,
we get caught in a self-perpetuating cycle of fear
begetting ignorance, ignorance begetting fear,
while bias and polarization continue to develop,
insensitively addressed, or not addressed at all.

As problems continue to fester unhealed
at the root of ignorance and fear,
violence erupts in the form of crime,
family violence and child abuse, drug addiction, gang warfare,
police brutality, rape, racial intolerance,
murder, religious and ethic antagonisms,
sexism, corporate crimes, riots and countless other societal ills.

For many, violence is the main language they have known,
and is the main way to express their needs
and vent their repressions.
Violence becomes an avenue to have your voice heard
and attain a degree of control or power.
Violence becomes a conditioned and habitual response.

Violence can also be the response of greed and be the means
to hold onto power and have your belief system stay in control.

Violence can be bred and perpetrated
from decisions and actions based on short-term
self-interest gained at the expense of others,
or the exploitation of limited or depleted resources,
to benefit the few.

When creativity is stifled, when dreams are thwarted,
when hope is lost,
frustration, rage and violence are often the resulting response.

Violence has its roots in deprivation and desperation.
Hatred is a cover for unfulfilled needs.
Eventually, the downtrodden and denied
will arise, demonstrate, rally, riot and revolt.

This is a pattern repeated throughout history, where political leaders entrench themselves in their offices of power, too often alienated from and in denial of the true needs and conditions of the people, unable or unwilling to communicate or address grievances, eventually respond to unrest with police and military action, escalating hostility and violence.

Nonviolent revolutions have had some successes in our recent history, but against the backdrop of our violent world, nonviolence as a way of life and means of social change is definitely the road most challenging and less chosen.

When there is insecurity in the basic fabric of society
and the cycles of ignorance and fear are perpetuated,
violence and war are often the habitual impulse.

We have war in our streets,
war in our hearts and minds,
war in our world.

War is how we torture ourselves
through our ignorance and fear.
War is the violent response to our lack of real security.

In the cycle of ignorance and fear,
as our societal frameworks are insecure,
ignorance begets fear,
fear begets ignorance.

Ignorance begets misunderstanding,
misunderstanding begets mistrust,
mistrust begets alienation,
alienation begets polarization,
polarization begets enmity,
enmity begets hatred,
hatred begets violence,
violence begets war,
war perpetuates insecurity
which fuels the fire of fear
and the continued cycles
of ignorance and fear.

To free ourselves from such cycles
we must exercise our creative choice
to make decisions and take action
based on the peace perspective.

We must take a stand
to uproot our ignorance
through educating and informing ourselves
so that our choices are based
on an accurate understanding
of all the variables to be considered.

We must meet and overcome our fear
by investigating truth
with an honest, open mind
in a nonviolent approach.

Human beings are not born violent.

Violence is an ignorant, gut-level reaction
in response to fear.

Nonviolence is
an intelligent heart-level response to love.
Nonviolence is an educated,
compassionate choice
in response to the world's problems
requiring emotional restraint,
correct information,
clear-minded intention,
spiritual empowerment
and appropriate action.

Nonviolence requires
power of conviction,
integrity of will
and unwavering faith.

Nonviolence is not passivity,
cowardice, weakness, appeasement or giving up,
but fearlessness, discipline, patience,
perseverance and an unending belief
in the inherent good in human nature.

We are all born children of God,
innocent and open,
blessed with unique and wonderful gifts to share.

There is no evil planted in the child's heart,
only life's universal quest
for growth and fulfillment.

It is only our acquired conditioning
of ignorance and fear
that leads us astray.

Knowing this, a Peacemaker reaches always
for that often submerged and latent good
residing in every heart
and finds a way to help bring it out
and connect with it.

A Peacemaker is willing to change for the good,
is open-minded,
is willing to accept criticism and correction
and to make amends for any misconduct or mistake.

Nonviolence requires equanimity,
balance and flexibility.

Gentle but sure,
strong but sensitive,
nonviolence yields but does not break.

This does not mean that a Peacemaker
should not take a strong opposing position
in full commitment to the cause
which he/she upholds.

Nonviolence not only requires
restraint and self control,
but also the release
of focused, well-directed power,
of positive thought and action
at the right time and place.

Diplomacy and facilitation skills
are effective tools of the Peacemaker.

A Peacemaker studies and develops such tools
and learns how to use them.

To be a Peacemaker it is imperative to be a skilled communicator.
It is only through communication
that the fires of aggressive confrontation, hostile reactivity,
abusive behavior and violence can be quelled,
grievances addressed and win-win solutions found.

A skilled communicator learns when to listen, when to speak,
when not to interrupt, when to make a point.

A skilled communicator learns to be objective,
when to hold judgment, when to make judgment.

A skilled communicator learns not to insist, blame or accuse
but to be clear, strong and centered in integrity.

A skilled communicator respects the one being spoken to
and creates a context for considerate, honest interaction.

To the Peacemaker, a skilled communicator
is centered in nonviolence.

A Peacemaker, to be established in nonviolence,
learns to still the mind,
be absorbed in silence
and be centered in an inner peace,
which brings insight, revelation and wisdom.

A Peacemaker may choose to study and practice various modern and
ancient nonviolent disciplines, spiritual practices and consciousness-train-
ing techniques, such as meditation, affirmation, prayer, yoga, movement
arts, exercise, body work, vision quest, relationship training, support group,
therapies and other modalities of change that help direct energy into a centered relationship with life's challenges and help establish the foundation
and experience of peace within.

As we become deeply established in peace
we reach a perspective point
where whichever way we pivot
we are at center, unified in oneness,
fed by all paths, faced by all directions,
surrounded by all approaches
yet able to focus on all sides
to respond to all changing views and challenges
with balance, strength and grace

From the vantage point
of this inner peace perspective
where we experience oneness,
the roots of peace take hold
and give firm grounding to our action
based in win-win, nonviolence
for the long-term interest
and the good of the whole.

And effective peacemaking is possible.

Practices: Restraint

Violence stems from unrestrained emotional reactivity. Restraint requires mental discipline, the discipline to catch and control your thoughts and emotions before you act in haste, in a hurtful, abusive or violent way. Restraint means to conserve your energy so it is used wisely, with appropriate power, sensitivity and positivity.

Restrain your anger, restrain blame.

This does not mean that you should not feel anger or not point out inequities or injustices. Rather it means you develop a control over your emotional reactivity and reroute that "negative" or potentially violent energy into an appropriate and effective response, well-timed and targeted towards a positive solution and win-win outcome.

Restrain yourself from the need to control, manipulate or dominate.

This does not mean you should not exert assertiveness or leadership when required. Rather it means you are sensitive to the needs and responses of others, giving others an opportunity for participation, delegating roles and authority, recognizing unique skills, abilities and input, whether positive or negative. It means providing a context conducive to creative collaboration and ownership. Effective leaders don't need to dominate but rather facilitate team-building to gain the sought-for outcome.

Restrain yourself from insisting. Practice acceptance.

Acceptance doesn't necessarily mean you leave things the way they are, but you accept what has already occurred, what is. You can't push the water back upstream. You can't change the past. From acceptance, we can move on and make amends. We seek to understand what has happened, moving beyond condemnation, blame or guilt to do what needs to be done now. When we insist, we impose. When we accept, we create a context of harmony and can come to forgiveness.

Restrain yourself from giving your power away too soon.

Practice patience. Practice listening. Gather information. Focus your thoughts. Conserve and concentrate your energy. When you act, act precisely, without wasted effort. Measure, time and target your response with the power of the integrity of your nonviolent commitment.

Restrain your tongue.

Talk less, listen more. Make your words count. Speak honestly from accurate information, from heartfelt feelings.

Refrain from making others wrong. Practice nonjudgment.

This does not mean you should not make judgments or discriminate. It means you do not waste effort on what others are doing or have done unless it is relevant. Rather you focus your effort on what you need to do and take responsibility for your own actions.

When you practice such restraints, you will find a reservoir of energy and power building up inside you that you can call upon when you need to unleash its reserves. Through the power of restraint, your words and actions will have more merit and impact and your effectiveness as a Peacemaker/communicator will be enhanced.

Affirmations:

I am nonviolent in thought, word and deed.

I am able to confront constructively any problem or conflict

and achieve a nonviolent, win/win solution.

I am capable of recognizing my fear and choosing love.

I am capable of recognizing my ignorance,

and choosing to be well-informed.

I am able to change.

I am balanced and flexible.

I am a skilled communicator.

I am centered in peace.

Protecting All Life

To the Peacemaker all life is sacred.
Life is a gift and a blessed opportunity.
Every living thing is born with the inherent right
to grow and reach its fulfillment.

Life is our heritage. Life is our right.

To violate, pillage, pollute, threaten, abuse,
damage or destroy life is the antithesis of peace.

A Peacemaker protects all life by any nonviolent means.

Nonviolent action is service
in the protection and nurturing of all life.

To protect life means to protect the rights of life.

A PEACEMAKER PROTECTS the basic rights of every human being to adequate food, clothing and shelter and respects the dignity of each human being to pursue their chosen life within the lawful framework of society as a child of creation.

A Peacemaker upholds the right to life, liberty, the pursuit of happiness, equal opportunity for all people, and justice for the common good.

To protect the rights of all life is to protect all creatures, as well as to protect the Earth and its fragile ecosystem from violation, pollution and destruction wherever and whenever possible.

A Peacemaker believes in the inherent right of the people to address grievances and to oppose and change unjust laws and conditions.

A Peacemaker may do this through any nonviolent means including voting, petitioning, lobbying, letter writing, political- and social-action campaigns, marching, rallying, canvassing, striking, court action, passive resistance and civil disobedience.

A Peacemaker understands that voluntary nonviolent obstruction of existing law may result in legal penalty, incarceration and possible bodily harm and persecution.

A Peacemaker is prepared to sacrifice, suffer penalties, bear abuse and risk life in standing for the cause of peace and protecting life.

A Peacemaker believes no act of government or law has the right to dictate, conscript or force an individual to be violent.

A Peacemaker will refrain from using physical force, except in extreme circumstances, and then only in nonviolent self-defense.

What differentiates a violent act from a nonviolent act is intent.

A violent act has intent to harm, damage or destroy

A nonviolent act has intent to protect, nurture, heal and renew.

A violent act, such as a person attacking and stabbing another with a knife, has the intent of bodily harm or murder.

A nonviolent act, such as a doctor lancing an infection with a knife, has the intent of healing, protecting and saving life.

In both cases, a knife is wielded and used to pierce the plane of the body, but with completely different intent and results.

In the hands of the attacker, the knife is a weapon.

In the hands of the doctor, the knife is a tool of healing.

A Peacemaker will never bear weapons or engage in a fight with violent intent.

A Peacemaker bears no arms except those extended from the shoulders and open from the heart.

Although a Peacemaker always relies on faith in the inherent good in human nature, there may be instances, individual or collective, when self-defensive physical action must be employed.

Physical self-defense is physical opposition to violent physical attack.

Physical self-defense has no violent intent, only the protection of life or life-support systems.

Physical self-defense is used only as a last resort at the discretion of the Peacemaker.

If an individual or vital life-support system is attacked and the decision is made to act in physical self-defense (as opposed to retreat or passivity), a Peacemaker will resist or subdue the attacker to the point where physical violence is no longer possible, where harm or destruction has stopped or where retreat is appropriate, order restored or law authority becomes present and in control.

A Peacemaker does not use harsh, profane, violence-provoking language or gestures and makes no attempt to incite violence in any way.

In certain circumstances—as in public protest, nonviolent demonstration or acts of passive resistance or civil disobedience—a Peacemaker must be able to ignore the taunts and challenges of a hostile crowd by being disciplined and self-controlled and not responding in a manner that could possibly ignite violence.

A Peacemaker must establish a peaceful presence, a surety of purpose, an unshakable strength of will and a collective solidarity that will speak more of peace than any tension-filled confrontation.

In situations where tensions could be high, one challenge, one ill-placed remark, one provocative gesture could touch off violence or riot.

If arrests are made, nonviolent demonstrators should act passively or cooperatively.

Designated spokespersons and leaders, trained and experienced in nonviolent action, should be the ones giving direction and negotiating.

The power of collective love, just cause, surety of purpose and unity will make the most impactful impression on the doubters, cynics and opposition.

A Peacemaker does not seek dominance or power over others to manipulate circumstance for selfish motive or look to gain advantage or profit at the expense and exploitation of others.

A Peacemaker aligns with the moral and ethical values of unconditional love, of respect for all life, of nonviolence and protection of all life. Living from the peace perspective to the best of her/his ability, a Peacemaker does not indulge in, work or support by personal habit, participation, purchase or active employment any activity or industry which develops, manufactures, promotes or deploys tools, products or services which are by their very nature detrimental or violent to health and life.

A Peacemaker does not seek dominance over nature, but rather respects her power and resources and strives to live in harmony with her ecology and rhythms.

> There can be no peace on Earth
> without peace with the Earth.

From the peace perspective, environmental violence could be considered any act that is pollutant, damaging or destructive of the ecosystem.

Since the 19th century, as the industrialized nations developed, environmental violence has been widespread and devastating, sometimes inadvertently or unknowingly committed out of ignorance or zeal for progress. It has been, however, our rape-plunder-trample the Earth mentality that has been responsible for the environmental dilemma. It is precisely that consciousness that must be radically and quickly changed throughout society.

In comparison to the history of industrialization, the environmental movement is very new. We are just beginning to open our eyes to the changes we must now make. Environmental concerns must be the top priority on our critical list as the damage to our ecological life-support systems and to wildlife continues and requires immediate and effective measures of response.

The main lesson of ecology is the unity,
the oneness of all life.
Every part of an ecosystem is interdependent.
We all breathe the same air, drink the same water,
use the same soil, walk the same Earth.
We all live within the same biosphere.
There is no place outside our ecosystem,
no "away" to throw garbage and toxic waste.
There is no replacement for extinct species.
There is no replenishing extracted fossil fuels
or restoring the pristine conditions of old growth forests.
Everyone is responsible for our environmental mess.
Everyone is responsible for the task
of educating ourselves and amending our ways
through environmentally aware life-styles and actions,
so that we can have a future.

It is a biological fact that an organism cannot live in its own waste. The issues of deforestation, global warming (the greenhouse effect), ozone-layer depletion, pollution and depletion of air, water and soil, garbage and toxic waste, unwise and shortsighted energy policies and overconsumption compounded by a rapidly rising global overpopulation, are the critical issues of our environmental crises.

Government agencies, environmental organizations and any other "they" out there cannot do it alone. Individuals must realize that "they" are us. Our individual life-styles are the major determining factors for the health of the Earth and our future. Shopping environmentally smart; recycling, reusing and reducing; wise water and energy use; planting trees and becoming active in environmental groups and projects are some of the individual actions that add up to making a difference.

Of particular concern to the Peacemaker in the area of an environmentally smart life-style is diet. It is well-documented that a vegetarian life-style has a tremendous impact on environment, health and humanitarian concerns, not to mention on our animal friends.

The meat and related dairy industry is inhumane and environmentally disastrous. A primary cause of deforestation and topsoil erosion is forest clearance to create grazeable land for livestock whose cholesterol-ridden, pesticide-infested, antibiotic-pumped flesh provides expensive, unhealthy food for a small portion of the world's population. Millions starve who could potentially be fed with the grain grown on the grazeable land or with the grain now fed to livestock in feedlots.

Meanwhile, meat and dairy industry products contribute to heart disease, cancer and other health disorders. More than half the water used for all purposes in the U.S. goes to livestock production. Huge volumes of fossil fuel are consumed in shipping and maintaining the giant meat and dairy industry.

At the same time, invaluable oxygen-producing, life-supporting forest habitats are lost along with the wildlife who live there, as carbon-dioxide emissions from fossil fuel used in meat and dairy production contribute substantially to the greenhouse effect and our oil dependency is perpetuated. These are just a few of the disturbing realities regarding a meat-based diet, not to mention the cruel and horrifying carnage continually perpetrated against the animals in squalid, tiny bins and slaughter houses.

Peace with the Earth must also mean peace with our animal friends. The human arrogance that sees us as the supreme inhabitant of this planet could do well to learn from our nonhuman friends who have much to teach us—from the industrial and organizational ability of the ant to the magical intelligence of the cetaceans. We butcher, torture, enslave and bring extinction to our fellow living inhabitants, failing to see that such violence perpetuates the habit of violence in our world and pushes the danger of extinction upon ourselves.

The idea that we need to eat meat to be healthy and strong is an exploitation of the consumer public by the greed of the meat industry. A balanced vegetarian diet can provide all the nutrients we need to be healthy and strong. I can personally attest to this after being a vegetarian for more than 20 years.

A vegetarian diet, or even a small reduction in meat consumption, becomes a nonviolent, revolutionary act when you consider the following: it sabotages the oil industry by reducing our oil dependency; it undermines the pesticide, chemical additive, animal antibiotic industries by requiring less of these products in our environment, food chains and bodies and it also reduces violence against animals.

If vegetarianism could take place on a mass scale, it could force such industries to convert to alternatives (peace conversion) that would be environmentally safer, while at the same time we could replant the forests, feed the starving, slow global warming, reduce air and water pollution and stop the violence against animals.

If we are to any degree what we eat,
we cannot build a nonviolent, peaceful world
by eating the result of our violence.

A Peacemaker eats no food that has been violently obtained.

Ultimately the Earth gives unconditionally to support life. All her resources are the heritage that belongs to everyone on the planet, yet 80 percent of the world's resources are used by 20 percent of the world's population in the industrialized nations. This inequity, which divides much of the world into northern hemisphere, industrialized countries and southern hemisphere, underdeveloped Third World countries creates a polarization of wealth and poverty, of have and have-nots, of relative economic stability and instability. The industrialized nations have exploited the underdeveloped countries, extracting resources and building industries dependent on the continued use of those resources to the detriment of the health and security of the entire planet.

Our dependency on oil has produced economic crises, war and ecological disaster. Eventually our oil will run out, as will coal and other finite resources.

We must place as national priority, the continued research, development and deployment of safe, sustainable, renewable energy sources such as solar, wind, hydroelectric and synthetic fuels.

We must leave behind the nightmare of fossil-fuel dependency as well as nuclear power with its horrifying potential for more Chernobyl-Three Mile

Island meltdown-type scenarios along with unsolvable radioactive waste disposal problems.

Our competitive, selfish national interests, motivated by short-term thinking for the benefit of the few, results in extremely unequal distribution of wealth and resources. That, along with our cultural, societal and religious mistrusts, perpetuate a cycle of ignorance and fear. Add on the cloud of nuclear arsenal insanity and critical environmental crises, and we find our world in a tense, polarized state—a travesty of what life on Earth could be.

In our high-tech race to dominate and subdue nature, we have left behind our inherent relationship to the Earth, forgetting the sacred bond and trust to love and take care of our mother, to protect life and live in balance with all.

We must ask the deepest questions of ourselves now and open our eyes to the world of reality. We stand at a turning point, as time and disaster once again conspire to accelerate our moment of choice.

We must create a new economic base where industry and jobs serve environmental and human needs. Environmental concerns must be a part of all business decisions. We must develop industries that create jobs and business incentives in inner city and poverty-stricken areas, including repairing and improving infrastructures, developing sustainable energies, improving the quality of our education and arts programs, offering affordable health care for all citizens, cleaning up and beautifying the environment. These can be the kind of businesses that employ people's creativity, offer new directions and alternatives and give people a sense of ownership and pride in their lives and communities.

We have the technology, skills and creative power
to amend our ways, realizing

The Earth has given us everything unconditionally,
and we have taken, like a child at the breast,
drawing forth the sustenance of life
but we have outgrown our innocence now
in the cloud of our destructive military capacity
and our self-poisoned ecology,
our polluted society
and still we take,
not knowing how to give back,
while the Earth continues to give us everything,
unconditionally.

We have access to all knowledge
at our fingertips.

It is not so much what we don't yet know
that holds us back,
it is what we don't yet understand
and accept.

Practices: Participation

A Peacemaker is a participant in a proactive, positive way, contributing to the health and well- being of one's immediate environment and community, as well as to the world. When you participate in doing something to help protect life, you are actively contributing to solutions, rather than being a spectator or a complaining, judging and blaming individual.

Are you living an environmentally friendly life-style?

Are you living energy-clean and efficient?

Do you participate in and support
environmental organizations and other life-protecting groups?

Are you informed on community issues?

Do you vote?

Do you write to your leaders and newspapers
about your concerns?

Do you have a network of friends and
support team members to work with?

How we choose what we participate in depends on what is right in front of us. Immediate house and family concerns come first—then community and broader issues can be tackled.

Use your voice. Take a stand. Live by principle. Plant a tree. Tend your garden. Nourish yourself and your loved ones. Find your allies. Magnify your strength. Organize. Go for it. Do it. Participate.

Affirmations:

I am a protector of all life.

I am a guardian of life-support systems.

I am an active participant

in creating positive, healing change on our planet.

I am a significant contributor to solution.

I am a builder of a sustainable future.

I stand in total commitment to live in peace, health and well-being.

Make No Enemies

A Peacemaker is always
careful to distinguish
between what one does
and who one is,
between wrong
and the wrongdoer,
between the act
and the actor.

We must recognize that the act
is not the actor,
but only a role the actor is playing.

A person may be a carpenter,
but that is a role, a job
that is what this person does,
not who this person is.

So it is with all of us.
We create roles and jobs for ourselves
in our life-drama,
but we get caught
in identifying ourselves by our roles
rather than by our true nature—
who we are in essence,
in Spirit.

Our roles can help us fulfill our mission in our lives,
which is the path that ultimately leads us
to a deeper relationship and understanding
with that Spirit, our Divine Essence.

A Peacemaker always looks for that Essence behind the role,
the real soul in the actor,
the inherent good,
the underlying truth,
our oneness, our unity, our common heart,
our peace.

If we reach deeply enough within ourselves,
if we reach out honestly enough for each other,

we will break through the illusion of the role
to find our true selves,
to find the kernel of good that exists
even in those we have come to mistrust or judge as evil,
or call our enemies.

We are all brothers and sisters of the same family.

We are not enemies.
It is just our assumed roles
that may make it seem so.

Understanding this,
a Peacemaker opposes enmity
and makes no enemy.

A Peacemaker understands
that the actions people take
are influenced by their background, education,
cultural orientation, values, mental and emotional programming
along with the other issues of their lives.

To varying degrees,
we are all products of our environment and society.
Society cultivates certain values,
encourages certain choices
and creates roles for all of us to play.

A soldier is trained to think and act as a soldier.
A police officer, lawyer, nurse, doctor, bus driver,
computer programmer, teacher—whoever—
have all been trained along certain guidelines
to be effective in their roles within society.

We have all received the training and preparation
that begins with our childhood, our family,
our corner of the world.
As we grow up
we all seek our roles in society's script.

Our educational systems promote certain belief systems
and orientations towards life.
The media presents myriad values and influences.
Our religious institutions preach doctrines
of morality, spirituality and behavior.
Our political, social and economic systems
are determining factors in the qualities
of our lives and the roles we assume.

These predefined roles
make seeing things from the peace perspective
all the greater challenge.

Our society is extremely good
at emphasizing profit motive and in training us
to be goal-oriented and competitive.
Unfortunately, profit motive often comes
at the expense or exploitation of someone else.

We are a society of winners and losers
engaged in competition
which is sometimes ruthless and unjust.
We get caught in greed
and shortsighted decision-making
in our ambition to keep pace
and stay ahead of the competition.

The true meaning of competition,
based on the Latin word, competere,
means to strive together at the same time
for the same goal.

Competition can be friendly,
but we have created it to mean rivalry, opposition.
We are taught to be adversaries, combatants,
to pit ourselves against each other—
"may the best man win."

We are encouraged to be winners.
To win is to achieve success,
reach the goal, make it to the top.
Winners are champions, number one, the best,
the heroes, the conquerors,
the gold medalists, the stars.
We are pressured to win,
not just to enjoy the sport
and the challenge and learning that comes from it,
but to win at all costs.
Winning becomes everything.
We are pressured to win, not to lose.

And when we lose, we are not taught how to lose.
Losing is not easily or graciously accepted
in our competitive society.
The emphasis on winning causes us
to perceive losing as a disgrace, a lessening of our stature,
a rejection of our value as a human being.
As a "loser" we lose self-esteem,
our pride takes a beating,
we are embarrassed, broken.
In our role as a loser, we suffer loss of identity.
It is difficult for us to lose
with grace, dignity, respect.

We are not prepared to accept
or deal with loss, failure or mistake,
to see it as a lesson for which to be grateful,
an opportunity to grow and be inspired.

Instead we are encouraged
to get ourselves back together,
rebound from the debilitation of the loss,
"suck it up," and do it right next time.

We often come to be sore losers.

We resent the winner.
We build for revenge.
We come back up off the canvas
for the next round,
the next shot at the winner.

We create enemies of the winners.

And the winners rarely know how to win
with thankfulness, with humility,
with honor and respect for the loser.

Real "good sportspersonship" is a rare quality.
What we more often see in the winner
is the victor's role played out,
covering puffed-up pride or swelled ego.
What we most often see in the loser
is the good face of masked failure
while groping for a way to cope
or building for revenge.

The winners egos become inflated,
and they must now protect their winner status.
The winners' goal is to stay on top
as long as they can
and to keep down and defeat the losers,
often at any cost.

The losers, scratching and clawing to be winners,
are the enemy.

In the role as winners,
we often suffer the gain of arrogance and vanity,
and the self-serving misuse of power and position.

We play this game throughout our society
of competing factions, competing wills,
of winners and losers,
of haves and have-nots.

This competitive programming creates
an adversarial context for our lives and our society,
which in turn creates separation and alienation
on all levels—
separation of our different roles and affiliations
from each other, from nature,
from our own true selves.

We forget who we are
in the false identification with our roles
as winners or losers, victors or victims,
friend or foe.
We cultivate suspicion, envy, fear, hate.

We mistrust.

Real friends are rare.

We create enemies all around us—in school,
in business, on the athletic field, in our relationships,
in our politics, in our international relations.

We make a world of good guys vs. bad guys,
heroes and villains,
allies and enemies.

Most of our world still holds to a law of the jungle,
survival-of-the-fittest, dog-eat-dog, gunslinger,
conqueror, defeat-the-enemy mentality.
It is that mindset which threatens
the entire world.

As long as there are enemies
there will be no peace.

The enemy is not ourselves,
but the ignorance and fear that leads to enmity.

We pay lip service to such adages as
"Love thy neighbor as thyself,"
or "Thou shalt not kill."

Why is there such a chasm
between our ethics and our action?

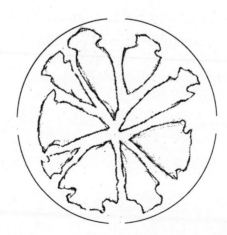

The answer can only be found if we look within,
in the depths of our hearts and souls,
in the harbor of our true nature,
behind the role, behind the personality,
behind the ebbs and flows of life's daily drama
to reach that refuge,
that full reservoir to which
all life's restless and meandering rivers run,
to which all the turbulent, troubled thoughts
retreat from their weary pace
and drink deeply of Spirit's silent strength,
drink deeply of the peace of perfection
with which all nature is created,
with which each soul surfaces
in perfection's image.

Then we know there can be no enemy
but that within ourselves
that keeps us from peace.

It is our own dis-ease
and our own ignorance of the cure
that keeps us from peace.

To see a fellow human being as enemy
and to fight among ourselves
is to fight the symptoms
which will never cure the cause.

The enmities, the hatreds, the violence, the wars,
the injustice, the inhumanities,
are all the surface symptoms
of a deep, well-established malady.

We allow our egos to create separation
and divisiveness.
We have been practicing divisiveness,
and that is what we get.
We practice war,
so war is what we get.

As long as we identify ourselves
by our separate egos,
by our roles,
rather than our essential, unified selves,
and we continue to go through life
attempting to satisfy this ego illusion
and false identification,
we will never be whole, never at peace.

We learn to equate happiness and security
with ego gratification,
and when another ego confronts ours,
and threatens that happiness and security,
we create an enemy, a win-lose confrontation.

We get caught in me vs. you,
us vs. them,
and we place blame on each other.

In reality we have no one to blame but ourselves.

We forget to see how each of us has contributed
to the crisis we face.

We forget to see that our "enemies"
are really just like us, divine beings in essence,
wanting answers, wanting resolution,
wanting peace in the long run,
but assuming different roles and approaches.

Our polarization becomes magnified
if we allow our egos to remain threatened
and our desire for ego gratification to increase
in the excitement and heat of the battle.

In defense of our ego,
we create such alienating emotions as
paranoia, anger, resentment,
hate, rage, fear, revenge.
When the fear level increases
and the conflict becomes intolerable
we lose restraint, lash out, strike back,
attack our enemies.
In essence, we are only attacking ourselves.

We are only hungering to retrieve our own essence,
the peace waiting and hidden deep inside us
that we knew as little children
in innocence and purity,
in our moments of play,
but that is now lost in the ego illusion,
in the enmity we have created.

The enemy is the problem we face,
not each other.
The enemy is the ignorance we face,
not each other.
The enemy is the fear we face,
not each other.
The enemy is the conflict we face,
not each other.

To handle the problem,
we must each take responsibility for our predicament.
When we learn to manage the conflict within ourselves,
then we can deal better with our mutual problems.

When we make our choices through the peace perspective,
then together, in the spirit of us,
we can express our creative problem-solving
for our mutual benefit.

To be whole we must practice wholeness.

To be at peace we must practice peace.

The world will never satisfy our hunger.
We will always be hungry again.

The world will always present an enemy
as long as we create separation.

The world will always be disunited
as long as we are disunited within ourselves.

We will know no peace
but that which we know within ourselves.

Practices: Identify Issues, Not Enemies

Think of a strong issue or conflict you have with someone where you feel angry or enraged. Practice separating yourself from the subjective and personal feelings you have about the other person. Try to isolate just the issue. Write it down without opinion or judgment. Just list the facts in the conflict. What are you really arguing about? What is really the issue? What is the root cause of the conflict?

Is it manageable? Is it resolvable? Can we come to a new agreement? Can we agree to disagree and still move forward? Is there a piece of the issue that I need to let go? Can we also address our personal feelings and release our emotions in an environment of listening, honesty, understanding and sensitivity? Can we continue as friends, colleagues or partners in a positive context? Where am I withholding feelings or information?

Are the issues too deep and far-reaching to assess objectively ourselves? Do we need help, such as a counselor, mediator, mutually trusted friend or third party?

Are we tempted to walk away without a satisfactory closure or completion? Is this relationship worth the extra effort?

From a spiritual perspective, it is important to remember that you are OK no matter what, knowing that God's judgment of you is not personified in the words or actions of the one with whom you are in conflict. This individual cannot really violate the true spiritual essence of who you are. You are already whole and complete.

The issue is really one of a separating emotion such as anger, guilt or resentment. Anger, or any emotion, is only an energy. We can learn to utilize that emotional energy as a fuel for the creative- combustion chamber we have within. Practice restraining yourself from acting on the impulse—which could result in a regrettable event—but instead use the fuel of the passion that you feel to empower you forward into a satisfying solution.

When you are able to take responsibility for your own emotions, then you can embrace them. Anger can be your friend. Make it a tool to empower your creativity. Use it to create solution. Live in the solution. Be the solution.

Affirmations:

I have no enemy.

I am capable of controlling my emotions.

I am able to see the good in others.

I am able to see the good in myself.

I am able to recognize my fear.

I am able to heal my own inner conflicts.

I am able to analyze the issues of conflict.

I embrace conflict and create solutions.

Living by Truth

In each moment the world offers us an encounter with Truth.
In each moment the world offers us a face-to-face opportunity
to come to terms with Truth
through the eyes of our human condition.

Who am I? Am I listening to my heart?
Am I living my fullest? Am I honest with myself?
Have I missed the Truth? Where have I gone astray?
Is my ego-dance deceiving me,
keeping my deeper, true self from being reached?
Can I reach that deeper self, converse with it,
drink deep of its reservoir of wisdom, of spiritual strength
and know it, live it,
not just for a moment here and there,
but in this moment now? Forever?

When I feel my human frailty, my doubt, my fear, my struggle with the unanswered questions, can I tap that reservoir for sustenance, for Truth? Can I hear and speak the Truth?

My voice within calls me to Truth.

Truth is that which we most crave and most fear.

A Peacemaker is a seeker of Truth.

Truth is what is—
without modification, elaboration,
addition, subtraction.

Truth is being.

Truth is one.

Truth is breath, heartbeat, life force, essence.

Truth is the source of existence.

Truth is the eternal present,
the permanent, timeless here and now.

Truth, the foundation of everything
from beginningless beginning to endless end,
is found in every facet and act of creation.

Truth sustains the universe.

Truth knows no danger.

Truth has no fear.

Truth has no death.

Truth has no enemy.

It is only I
who makes my own enemies within myself,
who struggles with my own doubts and fears,
who ultimately denies or chooses the Truth.

Truth, the indisputable fact of life,
the universal tendency of life,
seeks to grow to a fulfillment
and a completion of life's cycle.

Truth is the life force in a seed
that, nourished by soil, sun and rain,
grows and diversifies itself
into roots, stems, bark, branches, leaves,
flowers, fruits and more seeds
that find their way to the soil
to grow again.

Just as there are many leaves,
none of which are exactly the same,
and many diverse parts of the tree,
all spring forth from the same essence,
the same source, the same oneness
and are modifications of that oneness.

We are all manifestations of that oneness.
that Truth,
modified and diversified through our unique individualities.

Honesty, justice, credibility, integrity and sincerity are all behavioral modifications of Truth, as are our weaknesses, inhumanities, shames, doubts, fears.

What we experience as "evil" or bad in us is really the result of our quest for Truth, wholeness, peace and love gone astray and are behavioral modifications caught in ignorance and fear carried out in the direction away from Truth.

We may be caught in our imperfections, those modifications away from the Truth, that tell us of our blemishes, shame, distortions, unworthiness, smallness, sin, ineffectiveness. We may allow ourselves to be caught in the illusion of a past "truth," which can distort our ability to perceive what is relevant now. These distortions capture our attention under the weight of the world and we get caught in identifying falsely with them.

Eventually as our identification with these distortions becomes solidified so that we see ourselves as victims of a cruel world doing us wrong, we become blind and lose sight of the deeper, underlying Truth. We create negative convictions that rule our sense of self and reality.

We see our reality as dim and dark as we create the illusion of separateness from Truth.

Our minds, trapped in this illusion and further qualified through the various filters of societal influences, see truth as dualistic and transient, so what appears as Truth to one person may appear as untruth to another.

The truths and untruths are given as many different names and descriptions as language can provide and are interpreted the innumerable ways that our minds can devise.

We get caught in argument over these interpretations. Conflicts and disputes arise, wars are fought and the Truth is further and further removed from our view.

> A Peacemaker understands
> that one can never be separated from Truth,
> that Truth can never be lost,
> only unrecognized, misinterpreted, misunderstood,
> forgotten.

A Peacemaker understands that the seeker of Truth, whose journey may take many turns and twists, who may be severely buffeted by the trials of life, will never be abandoned by Truth—it is always there when the seeker is ready.

> Truth is the underlying law.
> Truth is the basis of wisdom.
> Our honest self-examination and questioning
> will lead us to Truth.

As we are willing to confront the issues that plague us, we commit ourselves to find the answers and to live and practice what we discover and learn. We see that even though we believe what we believe today with all our heart, tomorrow may offer a new perspective for us to believe with all our heart.

We find that old convictions or old "truths" like "I'm not good enough" can be replaced and upleveled by new convictions and new truths such as, "I am powerful and perfectly capable of accomplishing what I want."

Our willingness to invest our effort in heartfelt trial and error process will see us through.

This willingness leads us to trust in the process of speaking and acting in the spontaneity of the moment. Coming straight from the heart helps us bridge the gap of the illusion of our separateness from Truth.

> Opening the heart leads to truth.
> Speaking the truth opens the heart.
>
> Our self-created separateness from Truth
> is the source of all misery, pain and conflict,
> but when we touch Truth, when we find Truth
> and Truth becomes established in us,
> it will guide us, heal us,
> so that we may know peace.
>
> Truth is the anchor
> as we sail the tossed seas of life.
>
> Truth stands the test of time and experience.
>
> Truth waits as we return to it again and again.
> We all must face it.

A Peacemaker strives to live by Truth in all thought and action.

A Peacemaker strives to serve Truth on all levels of living.

A Peacemaker is a shepherd of Truth.

I sense this call
to grow, to flow
to strive to know
a turn complete
a cycle whole
to tune my soul
to the ring of Truth.

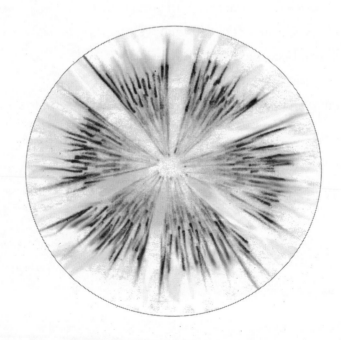

Practices: Living in the Question

Question everything, including self and authority. A question is a function of curiosity, of the desire to learn, of the quest for knowledge—a necessary step toward the truth. If we always ask, "Why?" Who am I?" What am I doing here?" then we will always see the world as an ongoing process, engaging our day-to-day exploration.

When we see the world as defined and fixed, then we ourselves become defined and fixed, rigid, inflexible, unable to accept challenge and change, unable to adapt as circumstances require. Truth may be one, but within that oneness are infinite variables, infinite options, choices, ways. If we accept just what we are told, without knowing in our hearts what is right for us, then we are on the path to being misled, lost and defined by someone else's limits and beliefs. We lose ourselves.

In our relationship with God, for example, if we accept blindly a doctrine of a church, then we are merely puppets manipulated by authority. If, however, we seek to know God in a real, living relationship, held in the heart and soul of the seeker, in the spontaneity and sacredness of the moment, then the relationship cannot be dictated, it must be experienced.

We must come to know God ourselves. We must seek our own relationship with God, just as we would seek our own relationship with our loved ones. This may or may not correspond with the doctrine of the church or the religious authority with which we are all familiar. The questioning process may lead us on a new, troubling or exciting journey. At least it will be a journey of our own choice, of our own self-reliance, and of our own authenticity.

This "living in the question," while it may seem unsettling, is really just the opposite because it creates an open-end to living, an open-minded rather than a defined, closed outlook. We become adjusted to the constancy of change, rather than polarized in inflexibility. We are open to improvisation and acceptance rather than fixity and intolerance.

When we live in the question, we are always in the process of discovering, learning, challenging ourselves. When we live in the question, we are always finding answers, creating solutions.

Affirmations:

I am willing to ask the deepest questions to know the Truth.

I speak and share honestly from the heart.

I release the past and accept what is.

I am willing to invest myself in sincere self-discovery.

I am open-minded and willing to hear other Truths.

I am able to know my Truth.

I am living my Truth.

Living by Love

As I live my life and move through
every day's array of experiences,
unless I ask my deepest questions,
unless I seek the answers,
not just to learn but to embody the Truth
then I may be missing a significant discovery—
that special moment when life has most meaning.

And so something in me compels me to live fully,
to have my senses reacting keenly and cleanly,
to be alert, awake, to feel,
to ask.

Have I taken the time to dance enough,
sing enough, play enough, celebrate enough,
touch enough, appreciate enough, give enough,
work enough, relax enough, enjoy enough,
love enough?

As I search through the maze of my life's journey,
and sort through and reflect on those moments of most meaning,
whether painful or joyous,
the basis of those experiences
of revelation and awakening, of understanding and insight,
of the answers to those deepest questions,
is love—
always love.

Love is the great teacher.

Love is the mortar of hearts,
the binder of souls,
the unifying force
and the creative energy in the universe.

We are all children of love.

Existence is the creation of love
and love is in the core of the heart of every soul—
only needing to be reawakened in those
whose hearts have become hardened and blind.

Love is the breaker of hearts,
the opener of hearts,
the mender of hearts,
the bridge between hearts.

Love is the sacred stream of infinite giving
through which Mother Nature
sustains and nurtures life.

Love is light and light is love.

Love is spirit and spirit is love.

Love is truth and truth is love.

Love is faith and faith is love.

Love is the sacred gift of life.
Love seeks only love,
cannot be possessed,
but is denied to none.

Love is the heritage of all souls.

Love is selfless,
but those who would covet love,
who would approach love with ulterior motive,
with lust or greed, with demand, insistence,
with control, with selfish desire for power or prize,
will deny themselves love's true blessings
and will experience restless sorrow and pain
until they come to know a sense of surrender,
until they come to know the opening of the heart,
the joy of selfless sharing,
of unequivocal giving,
which is Mother Nature's wondrous way.

Love is the pure joy of being alive.

Love is the power of salvation, redemption.

It is love that calls in the soul
to reach for the highest virtue,
for the purest ideals,
the truest vision,
for the eternal Truth.

It is love that comes in the moments of despair,
opens the heart and renews strength
and brings compassion,
wisdom and faith.

It is love that knows and feels
the depths of suffering
and suffers with us.

It is love that releases suffering.

It is love that releases bondage.

It is love that heals the deepest wounds.

It is love that calls for compassion.

It is love that asks forgiveness.

It is love that calls the soul
to open heart,
open mind
and be free.

It is love that brings surrender and release.

It is love that lifts the soul
beyond the limited self and bonds it
to the universal soul of oneness.

It is love that bridges the gap
of intolerance, hate, ignorance and fear
and brings us to universal vision
and understanding
and builds lasting bonds of trust and rapport.

It is love
that sends the soul soaring
beyond the earthly anchor
to the eternal abode of light and peace.

Without love
there can be no peace.

Love is peace.

If God be named,
may it be Love.

Practices: Giving, Receiving, Letting Go

In all interactions, whether "positive" or "negative," whether significant or insignificant, practice giving something unconditionally—a good word, a kind thought, a favor, a positive gift of some kind. The intent of the gift is what is important, not the bigness or smallness of it. Leave something of yourself that is connected to your true, loving nature. This giving unconditionally will help connect you with the love inside yourself.

Imagine yourself as a fruit tree and just give of yourself, of your fruit, as a gift to nourish others in some way. In doing this, even if just for a moment, you place yourself beyond the issues of separateness or the judgment of actions—or any "conditionality" for love. In giving unconditionally, you just love for love's sake, you just give for giving's sake, you just nourish for nourishment's sake, you just heal for healing's sake. In so doing, you give love to the world and help yourself and the world be a more loving place. The world will return the love to you.

Practice giving, not withholding.
Practice asking, not demanding.
Practice accepting, not controlling.

For love to thrive, the love energy must move through a circuitry of giving and receiving. This love circuitry is facilitated when we practice lovingly receiving as well as unconditional giving. We are all receivers of Divine Love, the creative energy of the universe. Do we receive with gratitude, with respect, with humility? Or do we just take and take?

Lovingly receiving implies an acknowledgment, an honoring, a thankfulness for the gift. It further implies a caretaking and nurturing of the value of the gift and an honoring and valuing of the positive, loving intent of the giver. It is not about being paid back, making a deal, signing contracts, owing favors, judging, expecting or being attached to outcome.

It is simply about allowing yourself to be a recipient worthy of love, capable of being blessed. It is about letting go of qualifications, conditionally, attachment.

Only when we are able to let go of the rigid hand of attachment do we learn to give and receive in these loving ways. Then we bathe in the glow of unconditional love which comes to us as grace. The loving energy of the universe will give its blessings. As we learn to receive the sacred gifts and be sustained and supported, we let go of our ego dance and surrender to the Divine Will.

All there is, then, is love.

Affirmations:

I am a giver and receiver of love.

I allow love to fill my heart and overflow to others.

I give and receive unconditionally.

I love and respect myself.

I accept love's healing.

I accept love's grace.

I love all life.

I am love.

Living by Faith

Faith is the inner conviction
that some greater intelligence,
some greater wisdom,
some greater force based in truth and love
is overseeing and guiding our actions
and our world and that we can work
in concert with this energy
to better the conditions
of our life and our world.

We all have faith to varying degrees,
but we don't always recognize our faith
and develop and use its power.

The power of faith is immeasurable.

Faith can be our greatest transformative tool.

Through faith,
the power of truth and love is potentialized.

Without faith,
doubt and hesitancy impede our progress.

Our faith can create miracles.

By keeping the faith
our dreams and visions come true.

Faith begins with a belief.

We all believe in something—
even nonbelievers have belief in their nonbelief.

This belief is not something
that can necessarily be proven by empirical knowledge alone
or by scientific methodology.

It is an inner or intuitive idea or feeling
that becomes confirmed as a belief
and strengthened through our observation,
experience and expanded awareness.

In our seeking and reaching,
our questioning and answering,
our process of trial and error,
a belief gains in its conviction
through continued confirmation of experience
and becomes a faith, an inner knowing
of positive, undeniable forward momentum.

The force of faith,
once we have committed to alignment with it,
can overcome any obstacle.
The force of faith is within all living things
and is that inherent movement of all life
to fulfill its potential and the completion
of its life cycle.

The force of faith compels us to actualize
our full beauty and power.

Once we align with faith,
we align with the very power of the universe
which cannot be understood by the mind alone.
If we rely exclusively or too strongly
on our mental reasoning,
on deductive or analytical process,
we may always keep a certain distance
between us and faith.

Faith is a feeling that does not rely on
analysis, reason, deduction, prognosis
or projection.

There comes a time when we learn
to release our reliance on reason,
to let go of structure,
to step beyond our comfortable boundaries,
our designed systems, our mind-sets,
our inhibitions, when we learn
to move through and transcend
our doubts, fears and insecurities
and enter what may be for us
a new, unexplored frontier of experience
and take a risk
relying on a sometimes-unexplainable, inner feeling,
an intuitive sense or conviction, a trust
that is connected to hope,
that is connected to the search for a clear vision,
a higher ideal, a deeper realization,
and then
if we allow it to be,
if we will it to be,
this faith can be as real to us as a mountain
and like the river which finds the only way
to flow to the ocean,
our power of faith cannot be denied.

Our first experience in life
is that of the power of faith,
that from the miracle of our very conception
we would move and develop
through the marvelous symbiosis
of the mother-fetus ecology of the womb
and grow from our embryonic beginning
to reach the moment of birth.

What force of creation,
what Grand Designer manifested
this incredible progression of life?

Surely it is beyond our power.

Surely despite all our scientific
and technological advances,
it is not explainable or understood.

Yet it is here, a mystery alive within us.

Surely even our high-tech wizardry
could never manufacture anything so beautiful
as a hand, an eye, a heart
or the mother-and-child relationship.

Surely we could never measure or quantify
the power of love or the force of faith.

And then at the moment of birth,
when we are pushed out of our warm,
soft, floated womb-home
into the harsh reality of the world,
whose command was it to come on out?

Who told us to open our eyes,
to draw our first breath,
to cry out in need,
to suckle at the breast
already waiting with nourishment?

And what directs each breath
after it has been expelled
to return again and again throughout a lifetime?

And where, at the moment of our last breath,
does life force, removed from the body, go
in the mystery of death's transition?

If we ask these questions to our minds alone
we cannot fully know the answers,
but if we ask these questions
in the depths of our hearts and souls,
we touch with and commune with
a depth of our being that knows...

That knows there is an answer beyond doubt,
beyond fear,
beyond reason or understanding.
There is an inherent wisdom
in the unfolding of the universe
that manifests itself through life,
through our breath and heartbeat,
through our window of consciousness
that is life's very essence and thrust
and that has been called
throughout the ages,
by the wise,
by the saints and sages
of various times
and cultural contexts,
in scripture, in psalm,
in poetry and song,
in exclamations
of inspiration and revelation,
the various names of God.

God?

One person names it God,

one person names it another God,

another person names it yet another God,

then argue over the word

and lose the feeling

and all these people are godless.

By whatever name

you may or may not call God

whatever your belief,

the feeling is faith...

It is faith that is found in the seed
that roots itself in the earth
with intent of the tree.

It is faith that extends itself
through the stem of the shoot and the branches
and reaches for light.

It is faith that embeds itself in the womb of the mother
with intent of human potential.

It is faith that cries in the voice of the baby
for nourishment, touch, nurturing, love.

It is faith that answers
in sun, in soil, in rain,
in care, in holding,
in providing sustenance
for the needs of life
in Truth
that life will grow,
that life will seek,
that life will find
through its eternal attempt,
through its undeniable will of being
the fulfillment of faith.

As clouds

spun by the wind,

it is without definition,

without name,

without beginning or end or now.

Graspless,

but nevertheless here,

it moves through and throughout

the continuum of its own creation—

high in the mountains,

deep in the sea,

everywhere that everywhere can be.

It has no birth.

It has no death.

It has no I.

It is free.

Practices: Planting Seeds

Take a pot, plant a seed.
Take yourself, plant a thought-seed.

It is not enough just to plant a seed. It must have nourishing soil, water, light. It must be tended. Then the force of faith will blossom as the plant grows roots, stems, flowers and fruits.

Similarly, every thought, every action is like a seed. It brings a result, and the result is potentialized in direct proportion to how it is planted and cared for. The more we plant and care for the thought-seeds and actions that are positive, life-affirming and spiritually uplifting, the more we get positive and uplifting results and our faith becomes strengthened. If you nourish the negative, harmful thought-seeds and actions, then you'll bear negative, harmful results, and faith will be crushed. You are your own garden. You are your own gardener. God provides us with all we need to have our garden flourish. Plant the kind of garden you want within the soil of your being. Select the seeds and nourish their growth.

Close your eyes and visualize your mind as a flower pot filled with rich, dark, deep soil. Select your positive thought-seed. Have it be something that is easily within your grasp, such as, "Today I will be more loving in my relationships," or "Today I will take time to ride my bicycle," or anything that will bring you a positive result. Imagine this thought-seed entering your fertile mind- soil and envision it getting the water and nourishment it needs as it grows roots and sprouts upward towards the light. This is your spirit rising, the creative energy of the universe being channeled through you, supporting and empowering you as the force of faith. Envision your thought, your vision, in as much detail as you can and take it all the way through as it grows into the best, most wonderful outcome. That is you. You are that.

When a negative, self-deprecating or self-defeating thought comes up, weed it out. Don't let it hinder, encroach on or take nourishment away from your desired thought-seed's growth. Be an attentive, on purpose gardener. Weed, mulch, prune, water, tend.

Your thought-seed will grow within you. It can grow beyond your wildest imaginings. It can become a powerful, transforming, healing force. It can change the world.

Affirmations:

I have faith.

I have faith in the power of love to heal and make whole.

I have faith in the power of truth to bring wisdom and understanding.

I have faith in myself, in my ability to know love, to know truth,

to know peace.

I have faith in the inherent, creative energy of the universe

to support and nourish all life.

I am nourished, I am supported.

I am whole, I am complete.

Integrity of Will

Faith and will go hand in hand.
Faith is empowered by will.

Will is the muscle of faith.

Faith knows there is a way.
Will makes sure it is found.
Will takes faith from the realm of the abstract
and moves it through action
into concrete realization.

Will is the courage
to make whatever effort is necessary to reach one's quest.
To the Peacemaker, it is the quality and intelligent focus
of that courage and effort
that must be enriched and uplifted
by a sense of integrity.

Courage is an inner strength
to face and move through ignorance and fear.

Effort includes dedication, education, preparation,
discipline, practice and action.

Integrity is living and acting with an honest, thorough and open reflection, examining and responding to life's challenges.

Integrity is standing in the Truth.

Integrity of will is the congruence of action with inwardly confirmed moral and ethical principles.

Integrity of will is a quality of living and choice-making that is based on heartfelt convictions rooted in love and truth.

Integrity of will is the ability to resist conforming to a mind-set, belief system or group mentality that does not correlate with one's inwardly felt principles.

Integrity of will is the warrior spirit to fight for what you believe in, even in the face of seemingly insurmountable odds.

Fueled by faith, integrity of will does whatever it takes to do the task at hand.

To act with integrity of will is to be powerful.

To be powerful does not mean to be manipulative, controlling, domineering, brutal or conquering. The peaceful use of power is rather the ability to synthesize successfully and harmonize energies and be decisive for the best possible use of those energies.

> Day-by-day living with integrity of will
> overcomes doubt, ignorance and fear,
> brings the strength to resist apathy, guilt or denial,
> defeats the temptation towards base and selfish desires,

removes the reactive pull towards hatred, revenge and violence
and keeps the Peacemaker on course
from the darkness of non-faith to the light of faith.

The world will always offer us a spectrum of choices, often difficult, per-
plexing, confusing. Integrity of will employs the wisdom to make choices
from the peace perspective—to know our true self, our oneness, to exercise
our yes and no with clarity, decisiveness and to use our power aligned with
the creative energy of the universe for the peaceful, long-term good of the
whole.

Free will is our creative choice-making.

Living in integrity of will is the merging

of our free will with Divine Will.

Divine Will is the power of faith working within us.

Divine Will always empowers growth and fuller expression.

Divine Will, through its creative energy,
is always producing change and transformation, as in nature.
It is therefore always creating something entirely new,
as in each moment, as in each new day.

Some people feel threatened by newness.
In our finite perception, in our bias, ignorance or fear,
we seek a sense of security
by holding on to that which seems tangible, permanent.
We do not always understand that changes are inevitable
or why changes are occurring.
We may become blind to seeing
how Divine Will is always working through us.

In our faith we know
that everything has a purpose and a meaning,
even if in the moment of tragedy, pain, illness
or blindness we cannot see it.

In our wisdom we know there is an answer
to the most puzzling and troubling of questions,
even if in the moment we cannot know it.

In our integrity of will
we hold on to our faith,
trust in the wisdom and our ability to understand
and reach deeply within
for the strength to carry on.

And the river of life will, inevitably, carry us on.

In the process of childbirth
the inevitable contractions are nature's helping hand
in pushing new life through the birth canal out into the world.
There is an inherent wisdom
in the design, facilitation and interaction
of this mother-child miracle.

Similarly, in every moment we give new birth to ourselves,
to our hopes and dreams, to our vision of peace.
In every moment, especially those of heightened significance,
we experience the contractions of the birth process—
our trial and error struggles, our pain, our joy, our loss, our gain—
and we see in our wisdom
that these contractions are the inevitable occurrences
of God's helping hand (Divine Will),
pushing and facilitating this new birth of ourselves
through the birth canal of experience into the reality of new being.

As in natural childbirth, if we tense up
with fear and anxiety, resisting the contractions,
we can obstruct nature's flow
and create more pain and distress in the birth process.
If we learn to breathe into the contractions as best we can,
to work in harmony with their intention,
we can relax and work with the creative energy of the universe
in a way that maximizes its ability
to carry on its life processes of birth and growth.

We learn to trust in the wisdom
of the natural flow of the universe.

We become channels for its power.

We become cooperators and cocreators
with the life force in action.

Divine Will initiates this birth process.
Divine Will guides this birth to grow
and reach its fulfillment of potential.
Divine Will is itself the inherent wisdom of guidance.

There is an integrity of will within us
that seeks alignment with this creative energy of the universe
and its Divine Will.

Through disciplined consistent practice
and use of our creative abilities
to open our channel,
to allow this creative energy to pour through us,
we can attain a degree of mastery
in continuing to facilitate this allowance,
to use its power wisely for the peaceful benefit of the world,
eventually to relax in its established presence and ultimately
to surrender to its Divine Will.

Surrender to Divine Will leads us to Truth.

Surrender is the releasing of fear,
the relaxing of the need to control,
demand or manipulate,
the trust in the wisdom and guidance
of the creative energy of the universe.

Surrender is ultimate faith.

Surrender leads to love.

The ultimate action of integrity of will

is surrender to Divine Will.

The ultimate act of creative endeavor is surrender.

The ultimate freedom is surrender.

Practices: Alignment With Truth

Choose a truth for you. This truth can be defined through any significant role you have assumed for yourself. For example: I am an artist, I am a performer, I am a father. These are indisputable truths for me, an identifiable role capacity. To practice alignment with truth requires that I choose one of these truths and then analyze and reflect on my relationship with that truth and make the effort to practice fulfilling this role to meet and serve that truth. To understand this practice, follow me through this example:

Say I choose father. What is my definition of fatherhood? What is my commitment? What do I know about child development? What do I know about parenting?. If being a father is a significant truth for me, have I fulfilled my potential in that role? Have I done my best? Have I satisfied my own emotional needs in this role? Have I given enough quality time to the children? Have I sought to understand their needs? What about schooling, peer-group pressure, home-based environment? Father overlaps with other roles such as husband, uncle, grandfather, et al. What are the requirements of these other roles?

Being a father is demanding. There are tremendous pressures and obligations wrapped up in assuming that position. There is an integrity of fatherhood. If I have accepted being a father, there is a will within to perform the role of fatherhood in alignment with that integrity. If I am out of integrity in my fathering, it will be reflected in my family's response to me, in my own response within myself. If I do not wish to be out of integrity as a father, then I must make the effort to align myself with what the truth of fatherhood is for me and perform accordingly.

I need to come to a defining and understanding of what the integrity of fatherhood is. Through my will to know, I make the effort to gain the information and insights about fatherhood. I practice the arts and skills of peace and employ the creative process in the role of being a father. I practice fatherhood in the everyday reality of family life. I get immediate feedback, immediate results. I make the effort to assess and reassess my actions. I make preparations, set goals, fulfill requirements, perform tasks.

If I take the position that being a father means taking responsibility for providing a loving, caring, safe and secure environment for my family, where every family member is nourished and encouraged to find their true gifts and make their own path in life and where I, in my father role, provide the services, duties and attentions that facilitate this to happen, then my effort to fulfill my sense of integrity is to perform my father role to the best of my ability. If I am aligned with my truth, living my integrity of will in the role of being a father, then I am at peace within myself. If I am not, my peace is disturbed because I am out of integrity.

When we are in integrity, life works well. When we are out of integrity, out of alignment with truth, life becomes out-of-balance and dysfunctional in some way.

Every role we assume has an integrity wrapped up in our participation in it. There is an inherent truth for us in that participation. Through practice, trial and error process, education and willingness to make the effort, we come to know that truth, align with it and live in that integrity. Eventually, through this integrity of will, we come to see our love growing, our faith strengthened and our guidance from Divine Will empowering us. Living in integrity of will leads to living in peace.

Summary of Steps in Practicing Alignment with Truth:

1. Choose a significant role in your life.
2. Proclaim and affirm the truth of that role for yourself, i.e., I am a teacher I am an artist.
3. Define the meaning and parameters of that role for you.
4. Analyze how well prepared you are to fulfill that role and what you need to do.
5. To fulfill that role is to live in the integrity of your truth. This can be facilitated through practicing the arts and skills of peace and employing creative process in any endeavor.

Affirmations:

I have the will to achieve whatever I envision.

I am powerful and prosperous and living my life's dreams.

I am a channel for the creative energy of the universe.

I am living in the integrity of my truth.

I am an instrument of peace.

I am guided by Divine Will.

I am that.

I am.

The Creative Process

The arts and skills of peace are the practices
by which an individual develops and employs the capacity
to open to the creative energy of the universe
and be an instrument of peace.

The arts and skills of peace are the practices
that ultimately lead to surrender to Divine Will. `

The arts and skills of peace are the creative processes
by which we make our choices, live our lives
and impact our world from the peace perspective.

The arts and skills of peace are the practices
by which an individual develops
unique creative talents and articulates those talents in a way
that helps establish an inner knowing of peace
and is of benefit to the establishment of peace in the world.

Through practicing the arts and skills of peace
we take our most ardently sought-for vision of peace,
health and well-being for ourselves and our world
and create that vision as our living reality.

The arts and skills of peace include
an understanding of creative process
and the practice, discipline and follow-through needed
to manifest that creativity
into a positive, healthy individual life-style
which also contributes to our collective, sustainable future.

The arts and skills of peace include a holistic approach
to practicing health of body, mind and spirit.

The arts and skills of peace
require the willingness, flexibility and openness
to change our ways of thinking and acting,
to adjust our choice-making to meet
the evolving needs of our rapidly changing world.

The arts and skills of peace
require each individual to accept responsibility for choices made
and to recognize that those choices affect not only ourselves
but the whole world ("act locally, think globally").

When we practice the arts and skills of peace
we open to the ability to recognize
and constructively confront our fear, ignorance, intolerance,

bigotry, injustice and find nonviolent means
to take action to heal and amend the situations that face us.

Divine Will supports each of us to flower and fulfill our life potential, no less than any plant or creature. When we consciously align ourselves with the creative energy of the universe, work in concert with it, merge with and surrender to its flow, then we know the wonder, the grace, the power, the joy, the well-being, the peace that is our divine heritage.

A peacemaker may define optimum health and well-being
as the realization of our human potential
fulfilling itself through Divine Will.

Our dis-ease results when we are out of balance,
out of alignment with creative force and Divine Will,
which may manifest as both sickness within our individual bodies
or the various maladies afflicting our society and world.

Practicing the arts and skills of peace
creates a context for good health and well-being.

Practicing the arts and skills of peace
creates a positive context for the establishment of peace,
and then for peace to be further studied,
understood, manifested and maintained.

We can never fully explain or understand why illness, tragedy, "accident," disaster or seemingly wanton madness occurs. It is a fruitless effort to try to explain all the "whys." All we can do is try, to the best of our ability, to extract what meaning we can from our experience, learn from it and in our ongoing lives accept what is and seek a sense of growth, balance and peace within ourselves.

There is no one way to come to this. There is one truth, but countless ways to describe it and countless paths to reach it. Each perspective may provide a clue, a key or a piece of the puzzle. Ultimately, only we can know the truth for ourselves. It cannot really be dictated or prescribed. It cannot be imposed on us from without. Only we live within ourselves and experience our own unique individual needs and outlooks. Only we can walk our own walk.

So it is each of us must assume responsibility for our own individual well-being through the choice of our free will. We can choose truth in the midst of a world which is tragically misled. We can choose peace in the midst of chaos. We can choose to love in the midst of hate. We can choose to nurture and foster good health in the midst of epidemics and environmental toxicity. We can choose faith in the midst of fear.

> We can choose to be an instrument of Divine Will.
> We can choose to create our lives
> as an expression of the art of living at peace.

None of this may be easy, but it is the choice and challenge of the Peacemaker. How we make our choices and meet our challenges is dependent on employing our creativity to gain the best results. Understanding the creative process gives us a handle to hold onto, a road map to refer to and be guided by.

Throughout history we have seen creative process employed for good or evil. Hitler used his creativity to empower a nation from a premise that was hate-based, which resulted in some of the most horrifying, tragic consequences in our war-torn human history. Gandhi used his creative genius to empower a nation from a premise that was love-based and in the process gave a lesson in peacemaking that is so deep and profound that the world has not yet been able to grasp it. The same could be said of the life and teachings of Jesus, Buddha, Mohammed, Moses, as well as more contemporary Peacemakers such as Martin Luther King, Jr. or Mother Theresa.

The saints and sages throughout history have all essentially said the same thing—we must respect, honor and enjoy our diversity *and* know that we are one. The creative challenge of the Peacemaker today is to break our addictive patterns and culturally ingrained mind-sets of intolerance, hate, bigotry, prejudice, greed, ignorance and fear—which is the legacy of the old paradigm of human behavior. The practice of the arts and skills of peace leads to the new paradigm based on love, cooperation, respect, interdependence and the fulfillment of our human/divine potential.

We have created a society of addictive behavior where we have programmed ourselves to support a pathology of hierarchies, power differentials, enemies, abuse, violence, dysfunction, cynicism and despair. We have created a society of hypocritical living where there is a tremendous gap between our professed moral and ethical values and our reality. We have overemphasized the mechanistic, scientific world view, which is logical, rational and empirical in its focus. This dependence on scientific methodology and technology has in many ways separated us from real healing, real vision and real creativity which must be balanced with our intuitive, inspirational and spiritual faculties.

Through the powerful and influential use of the media, we have glorified violence, machismo, sexploitation and abusive behavior. The gunslinger heroes ascend to the top of box office success and the message resounds to the public that to beat the bad guys and overcome adversity, punching out and blowing away people is the way to go. In a sense we have become addicted to war and violence as a means of resolving our conflicts. In this addiction, we have been unable to find our way out to a better way—to live the peace perspective, to live the art of peace.

Addictions keep us from ourselves. True creativity is the way we break old patterns and come to a deeper connection with our true selves. Without creative expression, we human beings suffer the disconnection of not knowing ourselves. The old paradigm imposes values from without and keeps us from our own direct communication and experience of truth. In the old paradigm we give our power away to an external authority that dissociates us from our inner sensing of who we really are. As we rely upon something outside of ourselves to connect us to truth, to show us the way, we lose reliance on our own inner compass and lose sight of our true direction. This is why there is such a disparity between our potential and our current reality.

The new paradigm springs forth from within and brings us to ourselves. This is why creativity is so exciting to us—it connects us to our inner inspired potential, to our individual unique gifts, to our full participation in life. The art of peace is about living a greater vision. That vision is based on the kind of premises and values that have been previously discussed. The creative process is the way we implement those values into our living reality.

Vision is what we want to do. Creative process is how we do it.

Creative process is about moving beyond limitations. It is about discovery. It is about learning, expanding, flowering. It is about freedom and the courage to risk, to explore. It is about practice, discipline and manifestation.

Creative process can be discussed in terms of the five "P"s—Premise, Preparation, Practice, Performance and Passion. All these stages have overlapping, internal and external components. The first, premise, is primarily inward in the establishment of internal philosophies, attitudes and visions that precede and are the basis for outer action.

Premise

The principles and values discussed in the peace perspective and peacemaker precepts provide broad moral, ethical and spiritual premises to use as a foundation and springboard for creative process in living the art of peace. These premises, or philosophical foundations, are formed in the cognitive intellectual portion of the mind (left brain). They provide an anchor to a matrix of values and understandings which give stability to the fluctuations and sometimes wild meanderings of the imaginative, inspirational and visionary aspects of creative process, which formulate primarily in the intuitive mind (right brain). When the values of these premises are accepted and established within an individual, creative process becomes a means of extension and interpretive expression of these values. The premise provides a structure, a basis to move from and improvise around, but the premise itself can also be open to modification and redefinition.

The beginning point or basic premise of creative process is the idea, concept or vision. A human being without vision is like a fish out of water, leading a pathless, hollow, dry life. But with vision and through the understanding and application of the creative process that drives that vision toward manifestation, our lives take on meaning, direction, enjoyment and satisfaction. With vision we move beyond fear and connect with hope, with transcendence, to a greater possibility. Then faith, waiting inside us, can spring forth and connect our power with the magic of dreams coming true.

Beyond that, there are some additional premises to consider:

The first is that *we are all creative.*

We may tend to think that creativity is only the realm of the artists, writers and great thinkers. We may put creative geniuses like Michelangelo, da Vinci or Einstein on a pedestal and devalue our own creativity by comparing ourselves to those who have achieved great accomplishments and recognition. We may carry emotional baggage that weighs down and blocks our creativity and keeps us thinking within limitations and smallness of self. We can be very creative in sabotaging ourselves.

The truth, I believe, is that we are all creative geniuses in our own unique individual ways. Extraordinary accomplishments are the results of "ordinary people" coming into touch with their special abilities. Through diligence and discipline, working with creative process, often empowered in the magical spontaneity of the moment, individuals discover and develop abilities to overcome their blocks and transcend the ordinary.

We all are gifted.

We are blessed with the creative energy of life pulsing through us in every breath and heartbeat. We are channels of creative energy. Like a garden hose with water rushing through it and a valve that determines the intensity and quality of the spray, we have a creative life force, a creative current, moving through us. The valve of our channel is our unique individuality which determines the nature of our interpretation, expression and direction of that creative energy, not just in a moment when we are doing something express-ly "creative," but every moment, all the time.

Creativity does not mean just the realm of the arts.

In the broad sense, *creativity is how we choose.*

Our choice of career, the way we dress, where we live, our prime relation-ships and how we eat are all determined by our creative leanings and deci-sions. Unless we are exceedingly well-rehearsed or bogged down in the exact same routines, the vast majority of what we do every day is made up on the spot as we go along.

Every conversation, every interaction
is an exercise in improvisation.

Every moment is new. Every moment we are using our unique abilities to choose, cope, give-and-take, judge. Every moment we are in a creative inter-action with life. Every moment we are engaged in the stream of life.

Every one of us is gifted with unique creative abilities. For each of us, there are activities or occupations through which those abilities are best suited. When creative ability is well matched with activity, we experience great joy and satisfaction because we are engaged in expressing the essence of who we are in the here and now. We are like the child at play—challenged, absorbed, learning, failing, overcoming, growing and lost in wonder, engaged in the pulse of life. The creative current is activated within us. We are turned on, excited. We are alive.

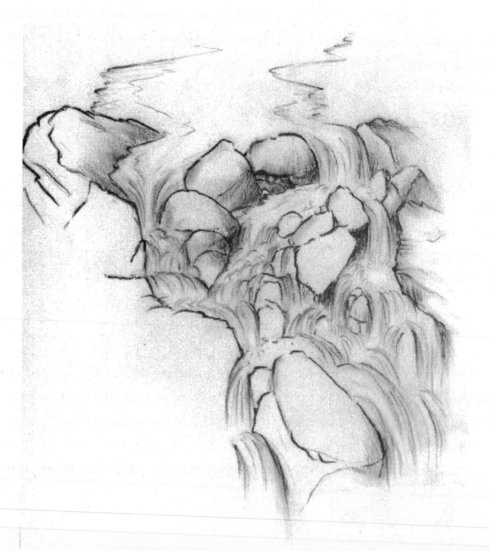

This aliveness is living in the *creative flow*. Creative flow is when both inwardly and outwardly we are engaged and absorbed in the process of expressing and manifesting a vision or idea which is directly connected to the essence of who we are. In the East it is called dharma, living in the Tao or the path. When we are living in creative flow, we are allowing ourselves to be naturally guided by Divine Will. We are working with the creative energy of the universe and our potential is unfolding towards fulfillment. Our spiritual evolution is accelerated. We are healing and moving on. We all experience this in varying degrees in varying moments or over extended periods of time. Why not consistently, every day, for a lifetime? This aliveness, this creative process, this living in the creative flow, is what I believe human beings are meant to do.

How do we know or recognize an activity or occupation that is right for our unique gifts?

We are naturally drawn to any activity which nurtures the heart and soul and opens the creative channel. If we are open, if we are alert, attentive and receptive, we will be drawn to it like a bee to a flower.

You know because it attracts you. It feels good. It feels right. It is where you belong. There is a resonance within that says, "Yes!" You might not recognize it at first, but it will draw you back again and again. It will capture your imagination. It will challenge your intellect. It will confront you in a positive, growth-enhancing way. It will challenge your emotional blocks and biases. It may evoke a fear in you that may call you to action. It will dare you to risk. It will offer you viable alternatives, new perspectives. It will open up new doors, new horizons. You will have a natural instinct for it. You will experience growth with its engagement in your life.

Above all, you will have a love for it and you will feel the creative current moving within you.

Creative process begins in the imagination. Imagination is stimulated by activity and in turn invents new activity, which further engages imagination and sets the creative flow in motion. Imagination is the channel for the creative current to move through the mind.

Imagination is the inventive faculty of the mind which makes things up.

Imagination is our mental ability to create images beyond the reality of what we are experiencing.

Imagination can lead us on flights of fantasy (positive or negative), daydreams, mental doodling. It can also lead us to great revelations, discoveries and creative endeavor.

Imagination is the "on switch" for the power of our inner creative mechanism. The creative mechanism consists of the initial imaginative spark, and the *creative capacity* to remember, store, nurture and develop that spark into creative flow which leads to manifestation. The creative mechanism is like the generator which keeps the creative current flowing and which needs to be understood and maintained to keep the state of creative flow going.

Inspiration, vision and spiritual revelation are the ultimate inner experiences of our creative flow. Manifesting tangible, positive results and service to humanity are the ultimate outer experiences of the creative process.

Depending on the individual, our creative mechanism has varying degrees of creative capacity. When our imagination is turned on and our creative capacity is open, the sky is the limit. When our imagination is turned on but our creative capacity is stifled by external circumstance and influences ("Don't waste your time." "You're not good enough." "Don't do that.") then we experience frustration. In this case we have an idea, but we can't take it any further because we are self-blocked or have succumbed to circumstances that we have allowed to block us. The creative current is dammed up, impeded.

In the moment of imaginative receptivity we are open and vulnerable and are very susceptible to influence. Children live in a state of imaginative vulnerability and the influences and emotional/psychological behavior patterns we carry with us from childhood have a direct correlation to our imaginative and creative capacity as adults.

Many of us carry wounds and scars from childhood that stifle our imagination or restrict our creative capacity and prevent us from living in creative flow. When we start to enter creative flow, the old patterns and the old fears kick in and we become blocked.

Creative flow requires an openness, a willingness to play, a freedom to release restrictions.

When one lives in creative flow, there can be a susceptibility to being vulnerable, to being jarred, hurt, dislodged or stopped in the flow.

There is a state of absorption and focus in creative work where one may temporarily suspend the connectedness to material reality.

We become lost in a creative, transcendental state. We become possessed in our focus. We are pregnant with possibilities.

In this transcendence, in this discovery of new territory, with unknowns involved and risks to be taken, it can be frightening and challenging. It can bring up all kinds of self-doubts, fears, self- consciousness, and confusion. Suspended in our creative absorption, we can become momentarily ungrounded, open and susceptible to intrusion or influence.

When imagination is turned off or negatively "inspired" and our positive creative capacity is limited or closed, then our frustration grows and we become "turned-off" human beings—cynical, negative, on a downer, with no outlet for our suppressed creativity. Our gifts have not been nurtured. Our needs have not been met. When our creativity is stifled or repressed, we often turn to blame, resentment or hate—which are really covers for unfulfilled needs, codes for crying out for help, for not being loved, touched, acknowledged or supported. We are stuck. We see no way out. As a coping mechanism or method of self-defense, our imagination becomes activated to create any protective mode of self-preservation that will work. We may live in denial, become passive, codependent and lifeless. We may learn to lie and manipulate. Or our self-defense may take the form of revenge, retaliation, abusive behavior, rage or violence.

Once these negative patterns take hold, our creative capacity can also nurture this negativity and we create dangerous and harmful responses to life.

But if we understand creative process, and keep it coming from the peace perspective, we can take the initiative to create for ourselves the right environment and influences that are positive, safe and supportive for our creative activity. We learn to protect ourselves in a grounded, affirmative way. We learn to create a balance and working rapport between a turned-on imagination and reality—which makes our creative endeavor tangible and measurable in our lives. This facilitates creative flow.

From our adult perspective we have the ability to keep our creative flow manifesting in a productive, serviceable way. Here is where it is important to have a positive and supportive environment for our creative endeavors.

We all have that inner child, innocent and imaginative, filled with the positive spark of life, who can be rekindled within us. Our inner child is the key to our creativity and joy of living. When we have lost touch with our inner child we get blocked in our creative flow.

It is never too late to rekindle our relationship with our child within and once again to be in touch with our open and vivid imagination.

It is in our imagination that we still perceive purity, wonder, infinite possibility and playfulness. It is in the imagination that inspiration has its roots, sparking the intellect, challenging the discriminatory faculty of the mind, utilizing knowledge and developing wisdom.

It is through the imagination, ripened and matured through the creative capacity, that inspiration leaps beyond the intellect and opens into the realms of spiritual awakening, healing, vision and faith.

Inspiration is the creative life force moving through us, which becomes translated through the channel of our imagination as an idea, vision or spiritual revelation. Inspiration literally means to breathe in spirit (from the Latin, in spire.)

To be alive is to be inspired with the life force that gives us heartbeat and breath.

We are all inspired.

We have daily aspirations and goals. We have short- and long-term dreams and visions and we have a far-reaching and life-fulfilling vision.

This deepest vision is directly inspired by Divine Spirit, guided by Divine Will as our spiritual destiny. This destiny is the fulfillment of the potential held in every seed to grow to its fruition. In human beings this fulfillment is supported by living a purposeful life with an on-course mission.

Our *purpose* is to express the quality of who we are in the deepest spiritual sense. Our purpose is not what we do, but is to express the true quality of our beingness that best reveals our unique gift *through* what we do. Our quality is our unique way of being in this world—such as being loving or supportive or serviceful.

Our *mission* is what we do to express our purpose and is the best blending of our unique creativity with activity. It is through the activity of our mission that our best qualities are expressed and we come to be "on purpose." Our mission may or may not be what we do for a living, but it is that activity which best leads to the realization of our vision. Our life goal is to express purpose, fulfill our mission and create our vision as our living reality.

Vision appears to different people in different ways. Some people are visual and see images three dimensionally while others may receive their vision in the form of a concept or thought. However it is perceived, everyone has the ability to envision and to act on that vision. Over time a vision takes hold in our consciousness and builds into something we feel drawn to pursue.

Vision is, however, always something that derives from within and is connected to an inner sense of who we are. In its deepest meaning this vision is a direct gift from Spirit and is guidance from Divine Will.

Inspiration, ideas, dreams, visions remain abstract and in our heads, however, until we move through the stages of creative process and begin to bring them out through action into tangible reality. This is where the crafts and skills of the artist come into play.

If we are inspired, then we bring it to life through the form, the medium, the style and the activity that we have chosen for expression. We combine our inspirational capacity with our cognitive or learning capacity, our right with our left brain, our masculine and our feminine. If our intention reflects the premises and values of the art of peace, then our creativity will inspire others and serve humanity in the quest for peace. But the manifestation of that creativity is dependent upon our ability to blend the different and opposing aspects of creative process that exist within, as well as without us in physical reality.

The physical world exists in a seeming reality of opposing factors: up/down, hot/cold, internal/external, masculine/feminine. Light is known by its contrast to dark. Freedom has meaning by its contrast to

bondage. In fact, creation in the physical world results from the marriage and combining of opposites. When masculine combines with feminine an offspring occurs and life reproduces itself. Masculine, feminine and all "opposites" are polarities of the same life force, projecting different and opposing qualities. Through the intercourse and combining of those qualities, creation produces new forms, new evolution. This is the creative energy of the universe in action.

Creativity is the ongoing marriage and combining of opposites within us.

Although each of us is predominantly male or female, we all have both masculine or feminine energy and qualities.

When inspiration sparks the masculine and feminine aspects in our minds to merge, an idea, a creative thought is born.

Imagination kindles the creative spark and the creative current is set in motion as a developing new thought-form baby.

Creative capacity is the womb for this developing new thought-form baby.

Inspiration fuels the continuing interacting and exchanging of the masculine and feminine energies within us in an ongoing continuum of pregnancy and birth, of nonstop creative current.

The new thought-form baby, born of inspiration and developing as a stronger and stronger vision within us, cries and demands to be further nurtured and developed.

As we serve this creative current and begin to form a more detailed vision through creative process, we enter into an absorption of the moment—living in the creative flow.

If, however, our masculine or feminine energy is unbalanced rather than in a harmonious flow of give-and-take, then our creativity may suffer.

If we describe masculine energy as projective, assertive, analytical and structured and we discuss feminine as receptive, nurturing, intuitive and abstract (which may also roughly apply to our left and right brains), then we can understand how the interplay of these energies plays a key role in creative process.

If, for example, we rely too strongly on our analytical power, we may lose an understanding or insight from the intuitive, or vice versa. If we are too assertive we could be like a bull in a china shop, or become insensitive, abusive or violent. If we are too receptive without appropriate assertiveness, we could allow ourselves to be stepped on, dominated, victimized.

The power of our creativity and its peaceful potential becomes maximized when these opposites within us become balanced and relaxed, so that their intercourse has a natural give-and-take born in the awareness, relevance and sensitivity of the moment.

There are times when either the masculine or feminine, or right or left brain, should or must be dominant.

There are times to assert and times to relax or listen.

We should be able to call forth and play either part when required.

A Peacemaker seeks balance of masculine and feminine, of left and right brain, of doing and being, of external and internal activity.

The Peacemaker comes to see the world not as a disassociated collection of random events and polarizations, but as an orchestrated whole united in the dynamic harmony of opposites within the continuum of creation.

Elements of Creativity

MASCULINE	+	FEMININE
projective	= CREATION	receptive
assertive		nurturing
definitive		intuitive
building		visioning

LEFT BRAIN		RIGHT BRAIN
logical		sensitive
analytical		feeling
linear		free form
system	*CREATIVE SYNERGY*	abstract
language		tonal
intellect		imagination
cognitive		inspirational

DOING + BEING
EXTERNAL + INTERNAL

YANG		YIN
hot		cold
hard		soft
dry		wet
bright		dark
defined		mysterious
active		passive

Preparation

When we awaken and tune into that continuum of creation moving through us and become aware of our vision, purpose and mission, then we are on our way to living in creative flow and achieving our dreams. But imagination, inspiration and vision are not enough. We must be prepared to move our vision into action.

Preparation means being ready.

In creative process, preparation includes education, finding and setting the right environment, building support and a support team, developing and acquiring the proper tools, achieving the right timing, managing our time productively and cultivating the correct outlook and attitude (being mentally prepared).

The way in which we learn, our ongoing education in and out of "schools," is a critical factor in preparing ourselves to fulfill creative process. In the previous section on premise, I discussed my belief that we are all creative, that we are all gifted with abilities and proclivities unique to each of us and that when we open to our inspiration, it will guide us to activities in which those abilities find expression. Those abilities are directly linked with our aptitude for learning.

We find that what we love to do, we also love to learn about.

We are naturally curious as a species and learning all the factors that are involved in our creative endeavor is part of the creative process. We need to know as many options and variables as possible so that we can make the best choices.

One way to consider education in a broader context is to see how a society provides a range of options. Where our options are limited, our creativity becomes limited. Since the nature of creativity is unlimited, and since the future of our world depends upon how we use our creativity, it behooves our educational system to be geared towards nurturing each student's unique gifts and combination of talents. This way each individual's best contribution to society can be maximized for the long-range good of the whole.

Unfortunately much of our educational system treats students like numbered empty containers, filing through a factory-like system to have those containers filled up with information that then gets spilled out on the next exam and is afterwards mostly forgotten. Learning becomes synonymous with memorization.

Students get divided up or grouped into different categories such as "gifted" or "less intelligent." These groupings are mainly based on a student's ability to memorize or perform on cognitive exams where those exams are often culturally biased. The whole person is not considered. These exams and other evaluation procedures often don't take into consideration other talents or degrees of skill or intelligence, such as body movement, athleticism, music and art, imaginative and intuitive faculties and other right-brain functions which may determine a student's uniqueness and special gifts.

When a student's uniqueness is disregarded, school becomes a boring place of drudgery where students do not relate to much of the subject matter and where creativity is undernourished and under-emphasized. When as students we close down to learning, we lose options and we risk losing touch with our creativity.

In our youth at school, we weren't always able to select our teachers, especially in the younger grades. We may have been far from happy with what we experienced. As adults, however, our power to choose a school, a teacher, a body of learning, a training now has a direct impact on our future, our livelihood, our creativity and our overall well-being. We are in the school of life and at some point we realize that we can no longer blame our past. We must take responsibility now for learning what we need to learn in order to create what we want to create. We must take responsibility for our own education.

Education means "to draw out," to inspire the student's love of learning by challenging the curiosity within.

Education is about stimulating the imagination. Everybody has the capacity for learning. We are all students. Education is about the excitement of learning something new.

To the Peacemaker, education is about integrating the whole person, the mathematical-logical with the spatial-creative, the interpersonal and the intrapersonal, the body and the mind, the masculine and feminine, the verbal and nonverbal. Education is about connecting knowledge with aptitude and developing a "learning flow" where the more you do what you have aptitude in, the more engaging and inspiring it becomes. This "learning flow," like creative flow where the imagination is stimulated, has a curiosity current that continuously entices, engages and challenges the intellect. We all learn differently and have different learning capabilities.

The learning flow happens when the right style of learning combines with the individual's unique combination of talents and skills.

For most students, this learning flow is facilitated when we are engaged in a task where it is not so easy as to be boring, and not so difficult as to be discouraging or frustrating. You continue to be challenged, you continue to learn, you continue to grow.

Learning flow and creative flow go hand in hand. They are inseparable and are the bridges between the cognitive and the intuitive, the left and right brain.

We learn as we create and we create as we learn.

One of the things we learn is that environment plays a key role and is usually the major influence in our creative process. We need to place ourselves in the right context, in the right environment to learn and to create. We need to build the right support team to facilitate our process and to have access to the right tools. These are part of the multiple factors involved in considering the impact of overall environment on creative process.

We need to select the right teacher and curriculum to help in our understanding and knowledge. The right teacher is a role model who exemplifies a degree of accomplishment, a life-style, a quality, a mastery that inspires and leads us onward in our own pursuits. It is extremely important in the learning process to have positive role models through whom we can see and have first-hand contact with the experiential result and truth of success in a field of endeavor.

The right teacher is one who not only has command of the subject matter and is skilled in teaching technique but is one who can express fascination and love of learning, invoking that same enthusiasm in the student, engaging the student in a curiosity flow and drawing out a creative flow in response.

The student absorbed in learning and creating embodies learning beyond just the cognitive level. The learning process becomes complete when a student experiences the truth of what is being learned on a visceral as well as on a cognitive level, in a creative response as well as a mental response. Environment plays a major role in our educational process.

Unless we live in a cave somewhere, isolated from the rest of the world, we are involved every day in creating the environment and series of relationships that have a direct impact on our learning and creative process. We come into this world as a family member. As we grow we develop additional relationships where we team up to support ourselves in creating what we want. Being part of any team involves being able to play the roles of both student and teacher. I learn from my team members and my family members all the time. I also play the role of teacher through how I express myself. In the midst of this teacher/student relationship, I express myself through establishing an environment which is supportive of what I want to create.

If, for example, I am going to create an album of music, I need to provide myself with a practice studio or place to conceive or compose the music. This needs to be a place where I am comfortable, where I have convenient access and which provides me with what I need, including privacy, sound-proofing, security and parking. In addition to my own musical background and training, I may need to bring in other collaborators, producers, arrangers, musicians, engineers, publishers, record companies, managers, graphic designers, promoters or marketing specialists. I am building a team. Together with my team members, I now create the environment of "we," where I play both the roles of leader and follower, student and teacher. I rely upon my team members for counsel and advice. We need to select the right recording studio at the right price. We need to draw up agreements and clarify our boundaries.

Team members are selected based on knowledge of their skills, a sense of personal and creative chemistry, respective background experience, track records and references. All along the way we are making choices which can make a big difference in the outcome of our creative process. We also have trial-and-error lessons, unforeseen factors arising, mistakes made, goals met or not met. We keep relying upon our individual and collective experience, knowledge and training.

Our ability to make things work for the best possible outcome depends on our willingness to be informed and thorough, to do our homework, to make good judgments based on a survey of options, maintain good team chemistry, develop the right attitude and follow through.

When our premise is clear, then the choices we make in our preparation reflect that premise. We select a style of music and an artistic presentation, we identify a market, we invent a promotion plan, we create an image. With clarity of premise, our choices can be made with decisiveness and confidence and our thoroughness of preparation breeds the sought-for results. The whole process of creating an album has a continuity, a solidity that manifests the original vision into successful reality.

The right attitude is often the key to success in any endeavor. Do we have the right attitude for learning? Are we mentally and physically prepared? Can we be a team player? What is our attitude when we face adversity? Are we open to different perspectives? How do we accept "failure"? How do we accept feedback? Can we take advice? Can we be taught? Coached? Are we afraid to risk? Are we willing to change? Are we willing to practice, study and work hard? Are we willing to play? Are we able to keep the faith? Can we stand true in our integrity? Can we let go? Can we accept? Can we surrender?

The positive *creative attitude* sees fear and doubt, challenges and opposition as realities of our world and, in fact, as essential and integral ingredients in creative process.

Everything in our physical plane has some element of resistance, tension and friction, even if it is minute. Otherwise our cellular structures would collapse. Even to stand up we must move against gravity. Without gravity everything would float away. Without the hardness and resistance of the stone, the sculptor could not chisel and render form. Without the resistance of the paper to my pencil, without the resistance of the table to the pressure of my hand, I could not write or draw a picture.

There is always an inherent tension or resistance that is natural and healthy.

In every moment we face resistance or obstacle of some kind. All of us face obstacles of various dimensions. The creative attitude sees these obstacles as challenges and opportunities for learning and for creative endeavor. Without a problem or challenge to face, without the need for solution, without the search for answers to our questions, we would have no need to employ our creativity. The question is not whether there is an obstacle to overcome or a tension to work with, but how to deal with it.

The creative attitude embraces a willingness to risk that nothing original or of significance occurs without a willingness to step forth from the comfort zone and take the plunge into unexplored territory.

Creativity is about discovery, not playing it safe.
Creativity is about exploration and improvisation.
Creativity is about working with and through obstacles.

The creative attitude embraces a willingness to allow for failure, to accept mistakes, to see that all experience gives its lessons in the path of learning, accomplishment and growth. Sometimes events that are the most painful are the most fertile for growth. Fear can be a friend if we learn to channel the fearful energy into a constructive, possible solution rather than a panicked, tension-filled reactivity. The creative attitude sees that fear can become an ally, keeping us alert, on our toes, engaged. So the obstacles and setbacks that occur along the way are contributing and enriching factors. Creativity is new birth and growth moving within, through and beyond old boundaries.

Creative flow is maximized when the time gap between idea and manifestation, between vision and reality is minimized. When we are able to catch an idea or vision that has a strong pull for us and rapidly enter into creative flow with it, moving deftly through the creative process to bring it into manifestation, it is an exhilarating and rewarding experience. We begin to see how our creative powers have unlimited potential. As we successfully move through resistance, obstacles and boundaries, we begin to taste how exciting, uplifting and liberating the creative process can be.

> When we are engaged in unimpeded creative flow
> we experience freedom.
> Freedom is the result of creating our liberation
> from restrictive boundaries, doubt, fear and limited vision.
> Freedom is being able to allow our vision to be fulfilled.

Freedom and its ongoing maintenance is the result of practice, discipline and learning. A dancer, athlete or musician cannot be free, graceful or effective in their form unless they have practiced, conditioned and toned the muscles, learned the moves and acquired the automatic dexterity combined with right understanding necessary to express themselves successfully.

So it is with freedom in our world. We cannot be free and at peace unless we are prepared, practiced and disciplined in allowing our creativity to be unbound by any chains, whether internally or externally imposed.

We create a sometimes endless list of reasons why our creative productivity is slowed, blocked or lost. Our often negatively conditioned language filled with buts, can'ts, don'ts, nos, won'ts, shoulds and shouldn'ts, backed by our emotion-packed demands, blames and reactions can define a stand or an attitude in our lives where we argue for our limitations, refuse to take responsibility and support reasons why we get stuck.

I'm Stuck List

I'm stuck because of FEAR:

of failure,

of letting go, of risking, of leaving comfort zone,

of others (mistrust), of self, of conditions,

of judgment, of rejection, of incrimination,

of exposing self, of facing truth, of reality,

of success.

I'm stuck because:

I'm a victim.

There's no time.

I procrastinate, I'm lazy, I get easily distracted.

I don't have the right environment, support team.

I'm too individualistic, not a good team player.

I'm not good at relationships.

I don't have the right tools.

I have no skills, no talents, no chance.

I'm trapped in armor, layers of negativity.

I'm caught in the system, the bureaucracy.

I'm weighed down by too many rules, regulations.

There's too much oppression.

I'm overwhelmed by poverty, debts, poor economy.

I have no budget.

I'm discriminated against, there's no opportunity.

It's everybody else's fault.

I'm a cynic, I'm depressed, I've lost faith.

I have no vision, no goals, no dreams.

I'm exhausted, I have poor health.

I'm handicapped.

I don't have the right background, experience.

I don't have the right education.

It's too frustrating, too difficult, too much.

I don't know where or how to begin.

I just can't do it.

I'm in a rut.

I start, but I can't complete.

I get hung up on details.

The follow-through is too difficult.

I can never achieve perfection.

The world is a hopeless, messed-up place.

In comparison to others, I'm no good.

My parents messed me up.

My programming got turned off at birth.

I'm a jerk.

I'm bad.

I'm probably dead.

We can all relate to these "I'm Stuck" stories, variations of them and many others particular to each of us. The question is, Do we allow ourselves to be blocked by conditions, whether self- or externally imposed or can we be in charge of our choices and our destiny? The more we learn and are creatively enrolled in taking responsibility for our choices, the more effective we are in living in creative flow. Then we are better prepared to survey options, improvise, adjust to changes and accommodate to sudden, unforeseen circumstances, conflicts, trials and tragedies when they arise, and still live in creative flow.

The key is to see these blocks as that resistance or those opposing factors which we need to work with and work through, which by their presence in our lives help us in developing the strength of our creative muscles and abilities. Any bodybuilder knows that strength gets built by working with resistance. As our creative muscles and abilities become more developed, then whatever experiences come, we are more seasoned and adept at handling them and making peace with ourselves and the world.

The trials and errors, failures and blocks become enriching factors, fertilizer in the soil of our Creative growth. We mix the experience gained and the lessons learned into the compound soil of our backgrounds and rich histories. This forms a positive and rich foundation for our roots to take hold and our growth and flowering to occur. As a result of embracing our fears and our blocks, and meeting the challenges they offer, our vision becomes more defined, refined and appreciated when attained.

Preparation means tuning and refining our creative muscles and reflexes so that we are ready to handle adversity in the best possible way and are poised to capture and nurture the visions and ideas when they come. The creative attitude takes responsibility for being prepared. Sometimes we are unprepared when an idea or inspiration comes to us. We might not be in a place or state of mind to retain it. It slips our mind, we forget it.

We must be ready. We must be poised to nurture the creative current, not to let it die. Ideas can be like dreams that we forget when we awaken from a deep sleep. Thoughts can flit through the mind like a butterfly that is here now and then gone when you turn around.

Have the butterfly net in your hands. Have your tools ready to serve you. Carry a notepad to write down your ideas. Keep a journal. Carry a pocket recorder to rap into, a pocket computer or laptop to help keep your ideas organized. Even if your tools are only a pencil and a restaurant napkin, a scrap of paper or your arm, write it down. Stop whatever else you may be doing and find a way to record the idea. Don't let it get away.

Develop your readiness to be receptive. Be open to inspiration. Be open to the imaginative spark setting off the creative current at any time, any place. Look for it to happen. Do research, collect ideas, gather information. Develop your memory. Survey the options. Seek challenges. Try something new. Meet new people. Build a network. Change things. Carpe Diem—Seize the Day!

The time is now, but our successful execution of creative process depends on the skillful handling of timing and the management of time with discipline and prioritization.

Being prepared means recognizing and taking advantage of the right timing. There are moments when it is most propitious to act or not to act. There is a season for everything. There is a time when conditions converge to support the most advantageous outcome, when the aspects are optimal for a specific result. As we prepare our attitude, skills, environment and tools, educate ourselves and survey the spectrum of options, then we are ready to move with a sense of the right timing. We come to recognize the significance of timely action, of precise and sensitive articulation and communication and we accept responsibility for choosing the time to act.

> The better we are prepared,
> the better we are able to choose the right timing.

Living in the creative flow naturally attunes us to a sense of timing. As we tune up our own creative mechanism, much like adjusting the proper timing and tuning of an engine, as we strengthen our creative muscles and stimulate the creative current to flow within us, we maximize our creative efficiency. This aligns us with the creative energy of the universe and we naturally find ourselves in the right place at the right time. Our improvisation in the moment convenes and concurs with the environment and circumstances around us to produce a synergistic, positive interaction.

Living in the creative flow is experiencing synchronicity with ourselves and our world.

Everything begins to work for us. New exciting options, new connections appear at just the right moment. There is magic. The universe is supporting us.

In order to get to this, however, a key part in the process of preparation is how we use our time—our time-management, our self-scheduling. Do we overload ourselves with so many things to do that there is "never enough time"? Are we stressed out with jammed schedules? Do we create enough "being" time or relaxation time? Do we efficiently plan our time so that we get things done, meet goals and still have time for recreation, socializing, family or intimacy? Are we so laissez faire or disorganized that we hinder our efficiency in getting the results we want? Do we prioritize what is really important to get done and discipline ourselves to take care of business or do we put it off and give in to other less important but momentarily attractive temptations?

Efficient time-planning, being on time, on schedule and being dependable are critical components of successful team-building and management. This builds a sense of trust. This facilitates creative flow.

A Peacemaker uses time wisely and efficiently, is on time and dependable.

The preparedness that comes from good time-management clarifies our ideas, develops strategies and brings results that enhance the efficiency of our sense of timing. If we do not comprehensively manage our time, if we are not fully prepared, when the opportunity opens to engage our input and give our creative gifts or to receive teachings and critical response we might not be ready and a golden opportunity can pass us by. So often things are left undone until the last hour, and then we suffer the stress of cramming to meet a deadline. Then we lose efficiency and relinquish a sense of comprehensive completion and follow-through. Our productivity is dependent on efficient time-management.

Efficient time-management helps build our preparedness in all areas of creative process, including developing a sense of timing in our communications: when to make suggestions, when to give feedback, when to listen, when to confront, when to take a stand, when to back off or release a position. A sense of timing—when a good comedian spaces phrases to maximize the laughter or when an actor gives life to the lines or when a musician plays the right riff, when a basketball player takes the right shot, when a good speaker brings the point home, when a good negotiator closes the deal—is an all-important skill that is the result of preparation, developed (as with all skills) through practice, practice, practice.

Practice

Practice is the extension of preparation through action and skill development.

Practice involves two main aspects: One is a consistently applied routine or ritual of body/mind/spirit disciplines to maintain health and well-being, such as prayer, yoga, meditation, tai chi, movement arts. The other is specific to professional or avocational activity, such as an art form, athletic activity, special project or business.

In all cases, practice involves some form of apprenticeship, student/teacher relationship, time spent with self in study, reflection and practice activity and time engaged with peers, students, friends.

A practice becomes your constant companion,
a best friend.
In the end, practice is the main process of learning
and leads to mastery.
A practice reminds you of who you really are,
helps keep you focused, on purpose, on course.
A master is a master of practice.

Through practice, our education becomes whole as we combine information and knowledge with their practical application in action. Only through practice do we gain the experiential embodiment of learning that confirms our faith and aligns us unshakingly with the goals of our educational and creative quest. Without practice, without the consistency of experience that practice provides, our learning is hollow, incomplete.

If, for example, we wish to learn to play the piano, we can read about piano playing and listen to and study the techniques of great pianists. Until we actually begin to practice and train on the keyboard ourselves, the result of realizing our goal to play the piano is completely remote.

Similarly, we can study the lives and teaching of great Peacemakers, but until we practice and actually apply, experience and begin to live the principles and modes of action that they taught, the chances of our becoming effective Peacemakers are nil.

In the area of mind/body/spirit disciplines, it is up to each of us to explore, find and choose which practices will work for us. Choosing the right practice is like choosing the right therapy with you as self therapist. Quite often, spending some time alone, practicing a discipline that brings inner peace, creative absorption and divine connnectedness can be worth much more than all the hours and dollars spent in a therapist's office.

Our practice should bring us a sense of joy and lead to tangible results. Ultimately our practice is that activity which we do and return to on a consistent basis which connects us to the creative energy of the universe and Divine Will and helps increase our well-being, health, fulfillment and peace.

> Practice is our access to mastery.
> Practice is our access to peace.
> Practice is our access to divine guidance.
> Practice is our access to surrender.

For myself, I combine yogic practices (postures, breathing, meditation), rigorous athletic exercises (running, ball-playing, bicycling, hiking), vegetarian diet, music and artistic pursuits, service-oriented activity and hopefully enough relaxation and "being" time to balance out all the doing in my career and business activities. I am also an avid backpacker and make it an essential part of my life to take one or more treks into a wilderness area every year. These have been my "vision quests," helping me return to and stay in touch with our intimate connectedness to Mother Earth.

Really everything we do is a practice. The way we eat, move, converse and think is all a practice that brings us closer or further away from peace if we choose to see it that way. We practice the arts and skills of peace every moment. The difference is the mental approach and consciousness we bring to each moment.

When our practice bears results, we gain confirmation and are empowered to take the next steps. Our mental approach becomes positive, and we accept the rigors of discipline, determination, consistency, repetition. We don't let conflict or fear block our way. We move beyond, "I'm stuck." Our will becomes the driving force.

Quite often the only difference between what we consider impossible and possible is the degree of focus, determination and willpower we put behind our effort.

Success in practice is dependent on the quantity, consistency and quality of effort applied to achieve a high skill level. No one wants to live with unfulfilled dreams festering inside. No one wants to live with unfinished business disturbing our peace of mind. Instead, through our will and the reliability of our practices, we keep the faith, knowing that the creative energy of the universe and Divine Will are undeniably supporting us every step of the way.

Practice leads to conviction.
Repeated convictions create mental patterns.

An idea or a vision becomes a conviction by constant repetition, impression, exercise, refinement, follow-through. When the mind and heart become attuned to the conviction of the good we are, of the peace that is inherent within, then we develop the unshaken conviction that is integrity of will fueled by the power of faith. There is nothing we cannot do as long as we believe we can do it.

As our practice creates positive confirmation within us and our creative flow becomes a living reality, we become like a flower reaching for an opening to the light. Our creative process leads us forward, around, over and through all fears, obstacles and blocks. As we grow towards the light, towards something to believe in, towards hope, we gain strength, skill and mastery. We heal our injured and broken parts that have held us back.

While it is important to recognize, analyze and confront our past traumas, blocks and fears, it is critical to have something to reach for to enable us to move beyond those old stuck patterns. We must create new mental patterns, new positive convictions that become more significant and meaningful for us than the old stuck patterns and which enable us to heal and move on. It is all important to avoid getting stuck and dwelling on the same old stuff that keeps us limited, blind and impoverished in spirit and self-worth. Through creative process there is always the choice to move forward. Through living in creative flow, we develop new patterns and convictions that support our unlimited potential.

The willingness to keep on track is an inner-driven process powered by our will. As we tune into deeper layers of inner confirmation and our conviction becomes affirmed, we sense a deepening connectedness to inner peace. This deepening and enriching of inner peace can be accessed through the consistent practice of the meditative arts, the use of prayer and affirmation.

Meditation in its simplest form is the stilling of the ordinary thought waves of the mind and is an absorption into the moment. Such absorption transcends self-consciousness, ego and worldly involvement so that the mind becomes a clear receiver for a direct link with Divine energy, without distraction. This process requires discipline and constant practice in developing the focus and concentration of the mind and the eventual relaxing of that discipline as one becomes established and freely accomplished in the meditative state.

If the body is restless and uncomfortable, if the mind is agitated, then the more difficult becomes the entrance into the meditative state. Mind/body disciplines such as yoga postures are designed to help make the body flexible, healthy and relaxed while keeping the mind focused, thus preparing for meditation. The more one is able to control and release the wild fluctuations of the mind and enter into stillness, the more one becomes receptive to inspiration, to tasting the inner knowledge of peace and to connecting to Truth and Divine Guidance.

There are countless techniques of the meditative arts which almost always use sound, an object or source of mental focus, a technique for quieting and relaxing body-energy and a relationship to breath. Each of us will find what form(s) of meditation and body/mind/spirit disciplines are best

suited for us. Ultimately, through meditation, the mind is trained to suspend identification with the body and senses; to stop perceiving the material world as the ultimate reality; no longer to become conditioned, addicted and tossed about as victim of our ego desires and the continually agitated state of the world. Through meditation, we enter into a deep and rich silence that is replenishing and connecting to Divine Source.

At the deepest level, the mind is pure. The pure mind is the reflection of truth, of love, of peace. The meditative, disciplined mind experiences peace as a living presence within, reflects that purity tempered by knowledge and wisdom and makes choices reflecting that peace perspective. Living in this peaceful alignment with creative energy and Divine Will, living in the absorption of the moment is meditation in action. When combined with the practical, external action-oriented aspects of creative process, our creative work in the world reflects and transmits our deepest, innermost intent and connectedness to peace.

Practice becomes a meditation in action. When through repetition and consistency we become accomplished in technique and style, trained in the fundamentals, we begin to transcend difficulty and struggle. Practice begins to become easier, more effortless. We become fluid in the form.

Absorbed in practice, we lose self.

Then there is just the activity. There is just the focus. The level of effort, concentration and discipline determines the progress towards higher degrees of accomplishment and eventual mastery. In mastery, practice becomes the continual returning and refining of the form which leads to innovation and new discovery.

Mastery can exist in a particular field of endeavor, such as a master mechanic, woodworker, cardiologist, schoolteacher. In this case, mastery means that through years of study, practice and skill development, an individual has risen to a level of expert accomplishment and proven excellence of performance and is regarded with high esteem as an ultimate representative of that field. This does not mean, however, that such an individual has achieved mastery of their life.

In the practices of the arts and skills of peace, where the whole person portrait of the Peacemaker is considered, the creative process involved in the achievement of mastery in a particular field of endeavor is also the creative process in the achievement of mastery of self, which includes the establishment of an inner knowing of peace. The premises and principles are the same whatever you do. The Peacemaker is always preparing, practicing and performing peace.

Life is a meditation in action. The goal is to be a master Peacemaker, living in creative flow.

In the arts and skills of peace we come to choose the activity through which our individual gifts can best be given. Through alignment with our vision, our mission is chosen and our true purpose is expressed. Our passion for what we most ardently want is not divorced from what we do or who we are. The whole person is in complete alignment with activity, so that physically, mentally, emotionally and spiritually we are being guided by Divine Will to reach our fulfillment. Hence, for the Peacemaker, the creative process of mastery in a specific field of endeavor is also the creative process of becoming a master Peacemaker. There is no separation between "work" and what we love to do. It is all part of the creative process.

Many of us are involved in *work* that we hate, that we regard as drudgery, that is divorced from our true creative leanings, disconnected from our vision, purpose and mission. The *job* is merely a means of making money. A key question to ask might be, "If I had all the money and resources I could possibly wish for, would I still be doing what I am doing now?" If the answer is no, then inner questioning and searching is required.

Our individual misery and the misery in our society comes from not being enrolled in doing what we would really love to do or not being engaged creatively or not feeling a sense of power, ownership or responsibility in building the lives we want for ourselves and for our families, communities and world. The creative current, the creative connection to hope, to a positive vision of the future, is blocked. When hope disappears, despair emerges. This is the tragedy of human existence.

Practicing the arts and skills of peace and employing the creative process build the opposite effect of powerlessness. By being clear and focused on our vision and purpose, our mission becomes defined and we create a right livelihood to support us. We may enter into a period of conversion and transition, where eventually we leave or spend less time in our old job as we create new avenues of enterprise to support us and we become more and more enrolled in our new direction. This may bring a risky, uncomfortable period into our lives.

But once we take a stand in the power of our conviction and follow our integrity of will, we step out in a bold, new creative direction that is self-empowering, self-reliant, infused with our passion for living and fully supported by the creative energy of the universe. Through confirmation in our practice, we know we are on the right track and there is no turning back. We find abundance, not only in just financial terms, but in a richness in life, in relationships, career, creative and spiritual fulfillment. Why would we want to do anything less? Why would we want to sell ourselves short? Why commit ourselves to misery?

When we find ourselves in difficulty, the healing and the answers are often found through prayer. Prayer is a sincere and truthful communication with God, Divine Will or whatever your sense or form of spiritual source may be. Prayer is asking for guidance, for strength, for healing, for solace and understanding. We can't ask God to solve our problems for us, to deliver the answer on a silver platter, to do it for us. But we can ask for help. We have been given everything we need, all the resources and tools, the know-how, the mind, heart and body to create a heaven on earth if we choose. We have misused our gifts, mismanaged our resources and tools, succumbed to ignorance, fear and greed.

Through prayer in our communication with God we can ask for forgiveness, for renewed strength, for the wisdom to see a better way, for the guidance to find the inner commitment and the inner strength to build a better existence for ourselves—to help ourselves and to help others.

In prayer, in realizing our own weaknesses, in admitting we cannot do it alone, we become receptive to input from inner guidance. Through prayer we open to an infusion of creative energy, of inspiration. When our prayer is spoken with heartfelt intent, with the openness to surrender to spiritual guidance, then our prayer is always answered. We might not hear a specific voice or message of counsel, but we might see a sign, a symbol or feel an inner confirmation or transformation occurring. Changes may take place around us. The teaching we need to know comes to us, perhaps in an unexpected way, perhaps not immediately recognizable, but a sign will show itself. The prayer is answered.

There are many forms of prayer: praise, devotion, gratitude, asking, confession, seeking truth. In any form, prayer is communication, and any successful communication requires a completed circuitry—of speaking, of being heard and being responded to. When we speak from the sincerity of our heart, with intelligence, honesty and sensitivity, in the right time and place we are always heard, we are always responded to, even if we cannot fully recognize the response.

Every sincere thought, every sincere request, every positive action brings a positive response from the universe.

Through the practice of prayer, the response within ourselves is a repatterning of our spiritual life, an opening to guidance and to the teachings, and a willingness to be receptive to inspiration, to revelation.

Through prayer we prepare ourselves to act creatively on
the guidance we receive.
Through prayer we are open to healing, to renewal.
Through prayer we know we are never alone.
Through prayer we are humbled
before the awesome power of the Divine,
and strengthened by its presence in our lives.
Through prayer we gain a sense of gratitude for the many
blessings we have received.
Through prayer we connect with the power of faith, with
the integrity of Divine Will.

Through prayer we are reminded of and connected to compassion and kindness in respect to our individual needs as well as the needs of others and all life.

Through prayer we are reminded of who we are and become prepared to accept the challenge of fulfilling our potential.

Through prayer our vision becomes defined and refined.

Through prayer we realize that the creative energy of the universe is supporting us, but we must do the action. In prayer we can ask for help, but we must walk the walk. Meditation, prayer and affirmation are inner-driven practices of the arts and skills of peace.

Affirmation is a practice of remembering and repeating verbal statements of positive conviction. A conscientious use of affirmations will help build a positive mental outlook and create a context for success in one's life. Affirmations are tools in a Peacemaker's arsenal of practices that can be used anytime, anywhere. To complete the cycle of creative process from vision to manifestation, these inner practices become invaluable support methodologies as we move into action in the external world.

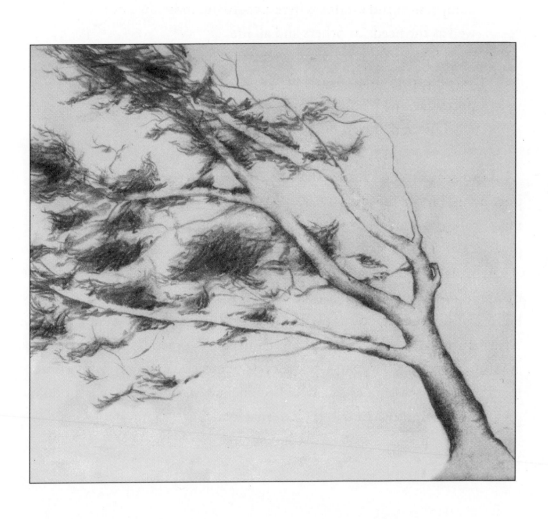

Whatever we do, the practice of the arts and skills of peace through the creative process in the external manifestation of our vision includes:

1. *Creating environment*—facility, support team, resources, network, finances, individual health and well-being, community health and well-being.

2. *Taking action*—practice, make drafts, prepare proposals, blueprints, sketches, plans, scripts and designs, develop, think-tank, brainstorm, prioritize, time-manage, put it into motion, do it.

3. *Accepting feedback, counsel, critique*—listen, take advice into consideration, be willing to move off a stuck place, consider another viewpoint, try to be objective, don't take artistic feedback personally, choose what is useful, reject what is not.

4. *Improvising*—adapt, adjust, accommodate according to circumstances, play in the unknown, be spontaneous, risk, change, move through "failure" and build on mistakes, learn from everything.

5. *Refining*—continue to modify, add, subtract, upgrade toward completion, work with subtleties, make sure the details support the whole project, smooth the rough edges.

6. *Doing your homework*—educate yourself, find the right teacher and body of information, research, survey options, know what to do when, how and where.

7. *Facing the facts*—assess reality, consider the practical framework, be honest, assess where you are with yourself

("Am I on target? Am I really doing what I want?"), consider timing.

8. *Following through*—take it all the way, give it all you have, complete the process, make sure all bases are covered, be thorough, perform your best.

9. *Achieving goals*—work step-by-step, confirm progress, affirm furtherance of vision, create success, experience your dreams coming true.

10. *Completion*—the vision is manifested, the project is communicated, the effort bears its fruit, the performance is consummated.

Performance

Performance is the extension of preparation, practice and skill development into presentation and communication.

Performance is the display of the evolvement of effort.

Performance is the exhibition of the degree of mastery attained, the living model.

Performance brings a tangible result, a gain or loss, a lesson, a response.

Performance is the consummation of a chosen form of endeavor in the moment of focus.

Performance is the on-line execution of action.

Performance results in a finished work, an ultimate achievement or an action in the direction of completion.

Performance is the sharing, serving, giving, the living expression of values and principles.

Performance is the manner in which we manifest our vision into reality.

To the Peacemaker, performance is the degree by which we live the arts and skills of peace.

When we prepare, when we practice, rehearse and refine our skills, performance becomes the follow-through of that effort.

Performance has a degree of perfection, of polish, of shine that represents a skilled interpretation of expression.

Performance is the giving and sharing of our creative process.

Performance represents the leading edge of our creative calling, the expression of purpose, the realization in process of our mission.

Performance is often the moment of highest achievement, of recorded value for others to experience, gain from and learn from in the future.

In the broad sense, we are all performers. Every interaction, every choice represents our performance on the stage of life. A teacher performs when giving a lesson, a parent performs the acts of parenting, a business person performs the acts of business, a surgeon performs surgery. We all perform our daily tasks, whether professional or casual. The degree to which our performance serves our vision, purpose and mission, determines our state of happiness, well-being and peace. It all comes down to performance.

Even though we may have completed an exceptional performance, the creative process is never over. The creative current within us is still flowing. It never stops. The artist is always in creative process. The performance is merely the crest of a wave. The inner calling, the motivation that sets the wave in motion, is still empowering us. The performance may have had a degree of perfection, a height of mastery, but to the true artist perfection is fleeting, perfection is relative, perfection is not an end. Perfection is the synchronicity of artistic intent with a moment in time. In the next moment, there is a new vision, a new guidance, a further motivation, a new wave forming, a new perfection unfolding.

What is the motive, what is the driving force behind our performance in the world? If we reap what we sow and the motive behind what we sow is selfish, ego-driven, power-hungry, controlling, exploitative or just off the mark and confused, then we will reap the same response in return from the world.

If our motive is based on the kind of premises and values of the peace perspective and the Peacemaker precepts, then we are performing on a much broader stage than the one of selfishness, ego-gratification or exploitative use of power. Our motive has an altruistic, generous, inclusive, positive and expansive dimension, as the practices of the arts and skills of peace keep us dedicated and connected to the path of peace.

Performance implies communication. Even though you may be reading these words long after the writing of them, these words, these drawings, this book is my performance in the moments of creativity. It is my communication through this medium of expression. Initially I am communicating with the inner voice of guidance with whom I have been collaborating and through this work it comes to you. Your reading and response is part of the communication circuitry. If there is something of value for you in these pages, then your life may reflect that, you may communicate it back to me or pass it along to others.

This is a source of gratification and satisfaction for me. Every performer enjoys an appreciative and valued response. Such responses are always inspiring and motivating. Every performer enjoys the affirmation of the work. The deepest motive for art, however, transcends the ego satisfaction of a round of applause or expressions of appreciation. It is inner driven. When the imagination is turned on and the creative current begins to flow, the artist is overtaken with the immediacy of the quest to express. There is a calling to give birth in some form to that expression. The creative flow is taking over. The birth contractions begin.

It will always be to some extent initially ego-guided, as in "I will speak to you. I will act. I will sing. I will share with you this expression—'my' expression." But as the artist is lost in the performance of the creative moment, that which is within, that which seeks birth, comes to life of itself through the performer.

The performer becomes just a vehicle, an instrument, a channel.

The valve of individuality and artistic skill gives it distinctive voice, but the expression, if it is truly inspired and charged with creative electricity, will take on its own living identity. The ego of the artist/performer is no longer a dominant factor. The ego dissolves in the art. The need to have it be recognized and applauded as "mine" is not as important as the pure expression, the communication of its value and meaning.

When art is divinely guided, the performer knows this guidance and learns to surrender to Divine Will. The performer in the moment of creative absorption is no longer ego-motivated.

There is something of much greater value occurring, something much more universal, something timeless, something unifying, something healing, something transcendental and freeing that is taking place. It is the Divine entering form. It is Spirit expressed. It is God's performance.

So the motive of the artist of peace is to ultimately surrender to Divine Will. To hear that Voice of guidance and give it form and expression takes practice, effort and then release of effort, release of ego, release of attachment. To such a one comes true wisdom, true mastery, true peace.

The heart of the performer is filled with the richness of divine inspiration and is humbled with gratitude.

Creativity is choice.

Choice is action.

Action is binding or liberating.

Action is binding

if its intention carries an ego-investment in the outcome.

Action is liberating

if there is nonattachment in the outcome.

If the action is performed as a selfless service, if the performer is a pure and open channel for the creative energy of the universe, if the performer is merely an instrument of Divine Will, if there is surrender, then there is freedom, then there is peace.

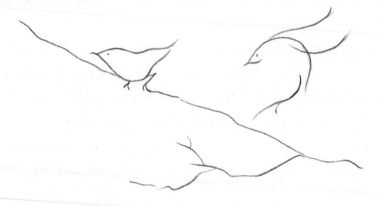

Passion

There is a creative energy in the universe that is all-knowing.
There is a creative energy in the universe that is all-loving.
There is a creative energy in the universe that is all-giving
and fully supportive of life to fulfill itself.

As we become conscious of and open to this energy
we begin to feel its presence in our life;
we begin to feel its guidance;
we begin to feel its current moving through us;
we begin to trust it, to work with it,
to access it on a daily basis, to follow its lead
and we feel within us a passion rising.
As a vision forms, a purpose becomes clear,
a mission unfolds—
a passion to see that vision become real,
a passion to give, to contribute,
to create a nurturing, sustaining, loving existence
for ourselves and for our world.

It is not a passion of greed, lust or selfish desire.
It is a passion like a thirst.

This drives us forward toward an oasis of peace,
toward a vision, a calling
where we satisfy our yearning for meaning,
by drinking deeply of the waters of wisdom
and the experiencing of truth.

It is a passion for knowing who we are
beyond doubt, beyond shame,
beyond fear, beyond ego
and for standing in the integrity of that knowing.

It is a passion for life.
It is a passion to employ our powers of creativity,
to see the vision of a peaceful, healed existence
for ourselves and our world be our living reality.

It is a passion to be free.

Let us come from our heart.
Let us go within and seek the answers
to our deepest questions.
Let us access the wisdom and guidance
of Divine Will,
so that we may see beyond
the momentary attractions and temptations
of the world,

that we may find the path through the minefields
of confusion, chaos and destruction,
that we may create and experience
a lasting peace
for ourselves, our world
and for future generations.

Let us commit with an undying passion
to the practice and the performance
of the arts and skills of peace
and to the employment of our creativity in our own way
to become master Peacemakers.

Let this passion empower our Creativity,
our quest for meaning.

Let us learn to harness this passion,
to channel this creative fire within us,
to inspire us forward and lead us
to quench our thirst for divine fulfillment, for peace.

If in some small way
these words and this book
have invoked and inspired
that passion to be kindled within you,
then my mission has been accomplished.

Practices: Envisioning

Close your eyes, take some deep breaths, be still, allow the every day thoughts to dissipate.

1. Visualize yourself in a moment in your past when you were most successful, most happy, most fulfilled. You may remember many instances, or perhaps just one or a few. Choose one that seems the most significant for you right now. Remember with as much clarity as you can what you were doing, where you were, who you were doing it with and what you were feeling. What was right about that moment? What was great? How did you do it? What led up to it? How did you participate in preparing and achieving it? This experience is not an exception in your life, relegated to the past, but an example of how your extraordinary abilities and gifts can become manifest, if you develop them and prepare the context for "miracles" to happen. "Luck," synchronicity and "miracles" are the dividend of preparation, practice and performance based on clear premises and focused passion.

2. Now visualize yourself in, the future, at a time when you are experiencing the fulfillment of your most ardently sought for dream. Allow your imagination to be free. See yourself in the moment of success, of magnificence, of greatness. Allow the creative current to flow within you. Allow yourself to be guided by Divine Will. Let go of your hold on

limitation or control. Watch the movie in your creative mind-screen. See yourself in the role you want, in the life-capacity you most long for. Visualize as much detail as you can. Again, What are you doing? Where are you? Who are you doing it with? What are you feeling? Know that this visualization is guided by Divine Will and is deeply connected to your positive, creative capacity. The vision you see may seem wild, completely out of reach or symbolic. Analyze it like a dream in which you are all the parts. See how it wells up from your subconscious and is connected to the true you—your purpose, your mission. Place it in the priorities of your life. Go for it.

Do this practice regularly. Develop these visions in as much detail and clarity as you can and then set them in motion through creative process. Keep the faith. Employ integrity of will. Channel your passion constructively, positively. You will achieve greatness. You will bring peace to the world.

Affirmations:

I create all I envision from a premise of peace.

I am an instrument of Divine Will.

I am a practitioner of peace.

I am a performer of peace.

I am peace.

The successful conclusion

of the creative process for peace

is based on the interflow and interdependence

of all aspects indicated on the flow chart for creative process.

Everything influences and interacts with everything.

Nothing is separate.

Flow Chart for Creative Process

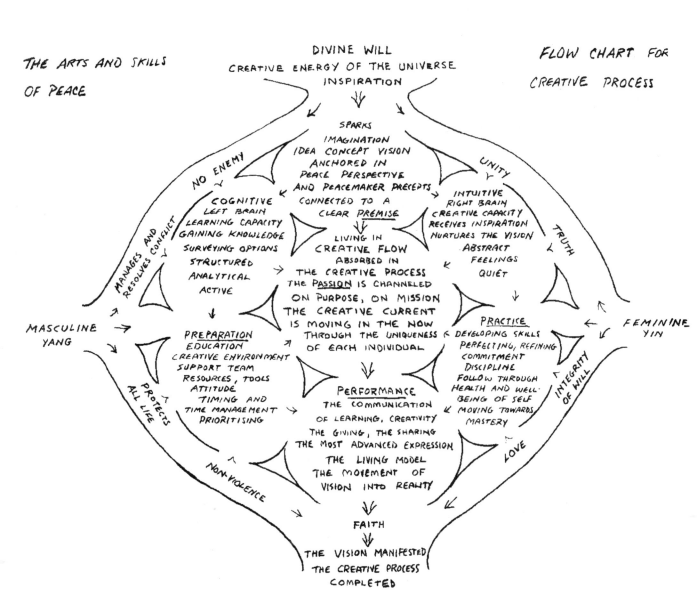

THE ARTS AND SKILLS OF PEACE

FLOW CHART FOR CREATIVE PROCESS

DIVINE WILL
CREATIVE ENERGY OF THE UNIVERSE
INSPIRATION

SPARKS
IMAGINATION
IDEA CONCEPT VISION
ANCHORED IN
PEACE PERSPECTIVE
AND PEACEMAKER PRECEPTS
CONNECTED TO A
CLEAR PREMISE

NO ENEMY

UNITY

MANAGES AND RESOLVES CONFLICT

COGNITIVE
LEFT BRAIN
LEARNING CAPACITY
GAINING KNOWLEDGE
SURVEYING OPTIONS
STRUCTURED
ANALYTICAL
ACTIVE

INTUITIVE
RIGHT BRAIN
CREATIVE CAPACITY
RECEIVES INSPIRATION
NURTURES THE VISION
ABSTRACT
FEELINGS
QUIET

TRUTH

LIVING IN
CREATIVE FLOW
ABSORBED IN
THE CREATIVE PROCESS
THE PASSION IS CHANNELED
ON PURPOSE, ON MISSION
THE CREATIVE CURRENT
IS MOVING IN THE NOW
THROUGH THE UNIQUENESS
OF EACH INDIVIDUAL

MASCULINE
YANG

PREPARATION
EDUCATION
CREATIVE ENVIRONMENT
SUPPORT TEAM
RESOURCES, TOOLS
ATTITUDE
TIMING AND
TIME MANAGEMENT
PRIORITISING

PRACTICE
DEVELOPING SKILLS
PERFECTING, REFINING
COMMITMENT
DISCIPLINE
FOLLOW THROUGH
HEALTH AND WELL-
BEING OF SELF
MOVING TOWARDS
MASTERY

FEMININE
YIN

PROTECTS ALL LIFE

INTEGRITY OF WILL

PERFORMANCE
THE COMMUNICATION
OF LEARNING, CREATIVITY
THE GIVING, THE SHARING
THE MOST ADVANCED EXPRESSION
THE LIVING MODEL
THE MOVEMENT OF
VISION INTO REALITY

LOVE

NON-VIOLENCE

FAITH

THE VISION MANIFESTED
THE CREATIVE PROCESS
COMPLETED

The Earth Verse

sung to the melody of The Star Spangled Banner

Oh, say, can we see
By the one light in all.
Our Earth to embrace
At the call of all nations
Where our children can play
In a world without war,
Where we stand hand-in-hand
In the grace of creation,
Where the rivers run clean
Through the forests of green,
Where the cities stand tall
In the clear skies of freedom.
Oh, say, do our hearts sing
For harmony and love forever
On the planet of our birth
Blessed with peace on Earth.

—*words by Stephen Longfellow Fiske*

Earth Verse is available on the Higher Octave Music album:
"Stephen Longfellow Fiske"
1991 Fiske Music/Higher Octave Music, Inc.

DURANGO STEELE

STEPHEN LONGFELLOW FISKE is a multitalented individual whose dedication to peace, environmental and humanitarian concerns has always found expression through his artistic pursuits. An award-winning singer/ songwriter, recording artist and concert performer, Stephen offers in The Art of Peace his talents as author, artist and peacemaker. A relative of the poet Longfellow, Stephen is a poet in his own right.

The Art of Peace is written from a wellspring of unique and rich experience. As Stephen has traveled widely bringing his music to events of social, political, environmental and spiritual focus, he has met and learned from many of the foremost thinkers and teachers of our time. This volume is a synthesis of these collected wisdoms—touched by Stephen's creative insights and poetic/artistic sensitivities.

A husband and father of three, Stephen has also been a yoga and meditation instructor, a seminar and workshop leader, an inspirational speaker, a record and video producer, a high school boys' varsity basketball coach, an events coordinator, a backpacker/mountaineer and above all, a student of the art of peace.

Other Works by Stephen Longfellow Fiske

Albums of Songs:

Seeds of Peace

Transformation

The Hundredth Monkey (Living Love Publications)

Touch

Funny Tunes

I Believe in You (A Fiske Music/Alan Cohen Collaboration)

Stephen Longfellow Fiske (Higher Octave Music)

Additional copies of this book may be obtained from your local bookstore, or by sending $24.00 per copy, postpaid, to:

New Paradigm Books
P.O. Box 60008
Pasadena, CA 91116

CA residents please add 8¼% sales tax
FAX orders to: 626-792-2121
Telephone VISA/MC orders to 800-326-2671